"*Fully Alive* is a stunningly raw book that breathes hope and life into the distressed soul. Susie holds nothing back, her words stemming from personal experience and girded with a passion to see God's people flourish. This practical guide will give you the tools and encouragement you need to face the difficulties of life, pursue wholeness, and believe God for a miracle."

—Lisa Bevere, *New York Times* bestselling author
and cofounder of Messenger International

"With every physical malady there are two battles: the physical illness itself and the assault on our minds—the doubts, fears, guilt, condemnation, questioning, and uncertainty about one's faith. Genuine healing is more than fixing the cells of the body. Genuine wellness requires healing the mind. Susie Larson has fought this fight, and through God's grace has discovered incredible insights that pierce the shroud of gloom, discouragement, and fear. *Fully Alive* will take the reader through simple steps that will free the mind, heal the heart, and improve one's physical health."

—Timothy R. Jennings, MD, DFAPA, author of *The God-Shaped Brain*;
The God-Shaped Heart; and *The Aging Brain: Proven Steps
to Prevent Dementia and Sharpen Your Mind*

"How do we reconcile the intersection of the 'already, but not yet' of our lives and persevere in the midst of suffering? Susie so beautifully and eloquently engages our hearts and minds to pray for a breakthrough."

—Jennie Allen, author of *Nothing to Prove* and founder
and visionary of the IF:Gathering

"As a counselor and woman who has struggled with anxiety and depression, I appreciate that Susie's message is practical and inspirational, filled with truth and tactics, and offers encouragement as well as empowering resources. God sees us as whole beings, and Susie shares His perspective in this healing, life-changing book."

—Holley Gerth, bestselling author of *What Your Heart Needs
for the Hard Days*

"I fix people. God heals them. Mine is an event. His is a journey. Susie gives us in *Fully Alive* a pathway to move from skin-deep fixing to deep heart healing.

As Susie states, 'What happens in our souls happens in our cells . . . dare to lift your eyes and trust Him!' Take this journey and grab your impossible healing!"

—Tom Blee, MD, trauma and acute care surgeon,
author of *How to Save a Surgeon: Stories of Impossible Healing*,
and founder and director of LIFEteam

"This book will change your life. Really. Because it's so much more than a book—this is like having a wise, tender spiritual guide walk you through the places in your life you most want healing and restoration. I'm cheering!"

—John Eldredge, author of *Wild at Heart*

"I'm often given the opportunity to endorse the writings of my friends, but none have touched me as deeply as this one. Susie takes us far deeper than wishful thinking and plows down beneath despair to plumb the wealth of all God has for his children. Don't rush through this one. Your soul cries out for the truth in these pages."

—Sheila Walsh, author of *It's Okay not to be Okay*

"If you're stuck, have unresolved grief, or are beaten down, prepare to be unstuck, healed, and lifted up! Susie will cheer you on every step of the way in this handbook for healing until you're full of fierce faith and holy confidence."

—Laura Harris Smith, CNC, nutritionist, author of *The 30-Day Faith Detox*
and *The Healthy Living Handbook*, and TV host of *theTHREE*

"Wow. Just WOW! *Fully Alive* truly is inspiring, educational, and healing. It fully captures the spirit of suffering and restoration. This book will serve so many!"

—Dr. Troy Spurrill, CEO of Synapse: A Center for Health and Healing

"As a physician, I am often struck by how spiritual and emotional blockages such as guilt, shame, and fear cause profound and distressing physical changes in one's body. Susie's book captures this complex dynamic between our physical health, our mental and emotional well-being, and our spiritual vibrancy. You will find great teaching, encouragement, and hopefully a path toward wholeness and wellness in Christ, our Savior and True Healer."

—Jimmy Ching, MD, Allina Health

fully
Alive

Books by Susie Larson

fully Alive

LEARNING TO FLOURISH— MIND, BODY & SPIRIT

SUSIE LARSON

BETHANYHOUSE

a division of Baker Publishing Group
Minneapolis, Minnesota

Published by Bethany House Publishers
11400 Hampshire Avenue South
Bloomington, Minnesota 55438
www.bethanyhouse.com

Bethany House Publishers is a division of
Baker Publishing Group, Grand Rapids, Michigan

Printed in the United States of America

ISBN 978-0-7642-3170-4

Library of Congress Control Number: 2018935307

Unless otherwise indicated, Scripture quotations are from the *Holy Bible*, New Living Translation, copyright © 1996, 2004, 2015 by Tyndale House Foundation. Used by permission of Tyndale House Publishers, Inc., Carol Stream, Illinois 60188. All rights reserved.

Scripture quotations identified AMP are from the Amplified® Bible, copyright © 2015 by The Lockman Foundation. Used by permission. (www.Lockman.org)

Scripture quotations identified HCSB are from the Holman Christian Standard Bible®, copyright © 1999, 2000, 2002, 2003, 2009 by Holman Bible Publishers. Used by permission. Holman Christian Standard Bible®, Holman CSB®, and HCSB® are federally registered trademarks of Holman Bible Publishers.

Scripture quotations identified THE MESSAGE are from THE MESSAGE. Copyright © by Eugene H. Peterson 1993, 1994, 1995, 1996, 2000, 2001, 2002. Used by permission of NavPress. All rights reserved. Represented by Tyndale House Publishers, Inc.

Scripture quotations identified NASB are from the New American Standard Bible®, copyright © 1960, 1962, 1963, 1968, 1971, 1972, 1973, 1975, 1977, 1995 by The Lockman Foundation. Used by permission. (www.Lockman.org)

Scripture quotations identified NKJV are from the New King James Version®. Copyright © 1982 by Thomas Nelson, Inc. Used by permission. All rights reserved.

Scripture quotations identified NIV are from the Holy Bible, New International Version®. NIV®. Copyright © 1973, 1978, 1984, 2011 by Biblica, Inc.™ Used by permission of Zondervan. All rights reserved worldwide. www.zondervan.com

Scripture quotations identified THE VOICE are from The Voice Bible Copyright © 2012 Thomas Nelson, Inc. The Voice™ translation © 2012 Ecclesia Bible Society. All rights reserved.

The information in this book should not be construed as prescribed health-care advice or instruction and is not intended to take the place of consultation with health-care professionals. The author and publisher disclaim all responsibility for any liability, loss, or risk, personal or otherwise, which is incurred as a consequence, directly or indirectly, of the use of and/or application of any of the contents of this book.

Cover design by Kathleen Lynch/Black Kat Design
Cover photography by Irene Lamprakou/Trevillion Images

Author is represented by The Steve Laube Agency

18 19 20 21 22 23 24   7 6 5 4 3 2 1

To my friend Lynn

Thank you for standing with me in the trenches, for lifting my arms when my own strength failed me, and for reminding me that victory and breakthrough won't come without a fight, but that after the fight, they will indeed come—because we are on the winning side. Your presence and persistence have been priceless to me. Thank you.

To Dr. Troy

God has given you a divine understanding of the human condition, and He's used you greatly in my healing process. How can I ever thank you enough? Thank you for your commitment to Jesus, to people, and to thinking outside the box. I thank God upon every remembrance of you.

To Dr. Jimmy and Karna Ching

God put you in my path at exactly the right time. Thank you for being such champions for me! I'm healthy and strong today because of your brilliant minds and kingdom hearts. Thank you. So much.

To my Savior, Jesus Christ

Thank You for allowing me such intimate and personal access to Your heart. Thank You for never giving up on me. Thank You for Your faithfulness. Anything I am or have become, anything I've accomplished, is always and only because of You. You are my greatest treasure. Can't wait to see You face-to-face. Love you so much.

Contents

Introduction

I N THE GOSPEL OF JOHN, Jesus asked a man who'd been sick a long time, "Do you *want* to be well?"

"I can't, sir," the man replied.

I've always thought I'd give a different answer.

I've recently walked through one of the most refining seasons of my life. Old health symptoms flared and new symptoms grabbed me by the throat. Anxiety surged and fear seemed to win the day. Current fears reminiscent of old threats instinctively made me curl up, cover my head, and brace for impact.

Day after day I felt prompted—strongly nudged, even—to revisit the passage in John chapter 5. But I couldn't understand why. *Of course* I wanted to be well. I ate well. Drank lots of water. Guarded a consistent bedtime. Prayed the Scriptures. Embraced faith. And took my vitamins. What more could I do?

Yet one day the Lord whispered these words to my heart: *"The storms reveal the lies we believe and the truths we need."*

I hated my storm. I wanted out of my storm. I couldn't bear the thought of another significant health battle surfacing and the anxiety it stirred within me. But once I realized that God intended blessings for me even in the midst of this storm, I opened my eyes and looked around. And though painful to face and to own, I soon discerned the lies that had held me back. Here's another important truth: *Those lies had remained hidden before the storm.*

Once I spotted the lies holding me captive, I also identified the truths that would set me free. Though I was clueless before the storm, I realized in the storm that I'd had my own "I can't" answers for Jesus' question *Do you want to be well?*

I know I'm not the only one. People everywhere are dealing with storms, symptoms, fears, rogue emotions, and anxieties that have upended their lives. A friend said to me the other day, "Dealing with emotional stress and crazy health symptoms is no longer just a topic for conversation. This is an epidemic crisis. People are stirred up, stressed out, and long to know the kind of health, freedom, and wholeness that Jesus promised us." I asked a couple of friends—one a counselor, the other a doctor—if they were seeing the same thing. Without hesitation, both answered yes.

The pressures of life, the pain in our past, and the stress perspective we choose all swirl around us, and even more so within us. There's not a woman who can honestly say that she's unaffected by it all. And because of the storm, we react—if not inwardly, then outwardly—to our hurts, our fears, and our perspective, especially if it's skewed. Eventually, our minds, bodies, and emotions suffer the accumulative effect of living an untended life in a stressed-out world.

I've learned a valuable lesson from my most recent storm, and it's this: *What happens in our souls happens in our cells.* A distressed soul creates a distressed body. Where our thoughts most often go, our lives follow. And the hurts and heartbreaks that we endure? They too will settle into our souls and into our cells unless we learn to metabolize them[1] with God's help and loving perspective.

We live in a culture that is addicted to treating symptoms. We want just enough help to get us on our way so we can continue to live a life of just enough, good enough, well enough. But at what cost to our souls, our story, and our calling—not to mention the very quality of our lives?

Something within us changes when we understand and live as though Jesus *cares* about how we feel. And He does care! He cares if our soul feels empty or if it's in distress. He cares if our body feels sick. He cares if our heart aches and if we just can't get a handle on our fears. He's with us on this journey. He's for us. And He wants us well. He says so Himself:

> Then Jesus said, "Come to me, all of you who are weary and carry heavy burdens, and I will give you rest. Take my yoke upon you. Let me teach you, because I am humble and gentle at heart, and you will find rest for your souls. For my yoke is easy to bear, and the burden I give you is light."
>
> Matthew 11:28–30

Scoot closer and revisit this statement: "Let me teach you."

There's a path for us to take where Jesus' yoke fits us perfectly. There's a place of faith for us to stand in the storm, where we'll know peace and strength where we once knew angst and fear. There's a promise written over our lives that compels us to dream about our future right in the face of our fears. There's a way to walk in Christ's light and easy yoke while living in a burdened, upside-down world. Jesus invites us to flourish here, right where we live.

Embracing the Mystery

I never ever thought I'd write a book on restoration, wholeness, and healing. Because, quite honestly, I've struggled with some of the theology that proclaims that God *always* heals, and if you don't get your healing, it's because you don't have enough faith. People said those kinds of things to me in my early years when I battled Lyme disease; not only were the comments not helpful, they were downright hurtful.

For years I've felt protective of those who've suffered long without a breakthrough. I've asked God to give them a gift of faith. I've asked God to protect them from people who sound like Job's friends and who assess the sufferer with the preface *You know what your problem is?*

Those who've suffered long don't need more ought-to's and should-do's. Those compassionless statements only make our burden heavier.

But the thing is, when we suffer long, we get used to our situation. We identify with it. And we lose our sense of expectancy. I know this well from personal experience.

It's in those places that we need hope and God's perspective. He doesn't leave us in our pain. He redeems us right in the midst of it. God still moves, still cares, and will do something in our situations that we never expected if we will dare to lift our eyes and trust Him, and if we'll determine to contend for the promise that He's put before us. God's promises are as potent as they've ever been.

And while I still believe that God performs miracles in our day, I also believe there's a mystery to this thing called life. Godly people get sick and die. Other godly people live but with disabilities. Two such people come to mind immediately.

Joni Eareckson Tada is bound to a wheelchair from a diving accident. She's even battled breast cancer as a quadriplegic. How much can one person handle? And yet, and yet, what God has done through this woman is nothing short of miraculous. How He has used her is downright breathtaking. And what she has suffered on this earth is nothing compared to the glory that awaits her in heaven. Scripture says so (see Romans 8:18).

I also think of my friend Jennifer Rothschild, who is legally blind. Last time we chatted I got the feeling that she senses she'll see her healing when she sees Jesus, and not until then. But when that woman speaks, God moves.

Both Joni and Jennifer are beautiful, brave, and bold—completely dependent on the Lord for their lives and their futures.

Though this book is about the broader topic of wholeness, restoration, and breakthrough, I must say, there's a lot of heat around the topic of healing. Those who've prayed earnestly for a loved one only to have him or her die are so deeply disappointed that they sometimes get angry when

> God still moves, still cares, and will do something in our situations that we never *expected* if we will dare to lift our eyes and trust Him, and if we'll determine to contend for the *promise* that He's put before us. God's promises are as potent as they've ever been.

the topic comes up. They're done risking faith on the things that matter most to them. And who can blame them?

Then there are those who've experienced a true-blue miracle and long for the rest of us to keep contending, keep believing so that we too will experience our own miracle. There's a part of me that feels very much this way even amidst some of my own not-yets, losses, and heartbreak.

You can see why this conversation almost forces us to choose one of two camps (and I've heard rants from both of these extremes):

- God always heals . . . if you have enough faith. And if you're not healed, it's your fault.
- God never heals, and those who think He does are spiritual kooks. False teachers, even.

Lord have mercy on us for the countless ways we've divided over theology that actually requires faith, a willingness to embrace mystery, and a heart set on the Father's love!

If you're willing, let's embark on a journey and explore Jesus' desire to see us flourish, to heal our soul, and to make us whole. Sometimes we'll get an immediate miracle, but I'd say more often, our healing-wholeness journey is more of a process. No matter what ails us— be it emotionally, physically, or circumstantially— God has more for us. We're not meant to stay stuck here.

> God has *more* for us. We're not meant to stay *stuck* here.

But to get unstuck, we need a sense of expectancy. Hope needs to make a comeback. Can we toss aside our preconceived notions and see if Jesus won't meet us in a fresh new way and even upgrade our faith? Dare we consider the notion that this kingdom life might be far more transformative than we once thought?

My recent heartbreak and health battle compelled me to dig deeper into God's promises regarding health, healing, and wholeness. I don't know that I'd say my faith has changed as a result of my most recent battle, but it certainly has deepened. I'm convinced—like never before—that God intends to do miracles in our day. I believe—with all my heart—that we'd see far more miracles on the earth today if there were more faith in our hearts. May God stir up a fresh gift of faith in us!

But I also firmly believe that there's a mystery to God's ways and that we don't dictate to Him; instead, we serve Him, honor Him, revere Him, and trust Him. Godly people get sick and die. I look at men like my dear brother-in-law Donny, or Nabeel Qureshi, the Christian apologist and author. Both of them died of cancer—far too young. But I now see that they won their battle. They didn't lose it. Cancer no longer grips them in its ugly, devastating clutches or robs them of health and peace. They're with Jesus—full, healed, and free. And our time with them will far exceed our short time without them.

I also remember my very first mentor and her battle with throat cancer. One day, with fire in her eyes and her handheld voice box pushed up against her throat, she said, "Susie, God is with me here. Don't you doubt that for a second. And He will take me when He can get more glory from my death than He does from my life."

I'll never forget her words or her faith. She lived a fruitful, faithful life. She lost nothing and gained heaven. The loss was ours. We miss her. But we'll see her again.

And there are those whose lot involves life with a disability. Such a cross. Such a cost. But God is with them, and He'll either miraculously heal them, or He'll miraculously use them in a way that allows them to flourish and reflect the Father's heart right in the midst of their vulnerability. Life on earth is short. Eternity is long. God's promises are true. And if you follow Jesus through the Gospels, you'll find a Savior who cares deeply about the human condition.

What, Then, Are We Called to Do?

That fact—our Savior's heart for the human condition—is what brings us the assurance that God wants us to thrive, and He's with us every step of the way.

You and I need to make some adjustments amidst the craziness of this world and the toxicity of our times. God offers us wisdom from above, wisdom that's unique to us and to our situation. But in order for us to know the fullness and the restoration that are possible for us as heirs of God, we have some things to learn. We cannot and must not keep grinding our gears through life while ignoring the physical and emotional toll that our hardships have had on us. Neither can we ignore the mental and/or emotional symptoms that are trying to get our attention.

I can't prove this, but I believe there's a trapdoor in our hearts that drops things into our souls. Our soul is the place where our emotions brew and our hurts collide, and the turmoil of it all can put the squeeze on our hopes, our dreams, and our perspective. Jesus wants peace to rule and reign in our hearts so that we can prosper in our soul. He wants us to flourish in every way possible.

> My beloved friend, I pray that everything is going well for you and that your body is as healthy as your soul is prosperous.
>
> 3 John 1:2 THE VOICE

So here's what we're going to do on this journey:

We're going to pursue wholeness.
And we're going to pray for a miracle.

We're going to ask God for a fresh vision of what flourishing can look like for us, and then we're going to position ourselves on the path of healing—whatever it takes. Some of this will be hard. But you're no stranger to hard. You've done it before. We can do hard if it leads us to a better life, right? We're going to roll up our sleeves, take inventory of our habits, give our soul some room to breathe, and maybe change a few of our ways so we can enjoy better health.

And then we're going to go before the Most High God, who loves us with a passion we cannot fathom, and we're going to ask Him for a miracle, because He's the same God yesterday, today, and forever. He loves us, and He still performs miracles today.

Maybe yours is an emotional miracle. You want to be delivered from the constant stress of being at the mercy of your roller-coaster emotions.

You're going to do the work of renewing your thoughts and of standing on God's promises. You're going to get at the root cause of your fears. Then you're going to ask God to do what only He can do. Imagine what a miracle might look like in your life. Do you believe God can and wants to intervene on your behalf?

Maybe yours is a physical miracle. You've suffered a long time. And though you're weary, you're not giving up. You're about to make some adjustments that might just be game-changers for you. You're about to learn how to separate your emotions from your symptoms. You're about to build a new infrastructure in your thought life. And together, we're going to err on the side of faith for you, and ask God to do what only He can do.

Maybe yours is a relational miracle. Your heartbreak has taken a toll on your soul. Are you ready to give Jesus access to your heartbreak and disappointment? Are you ready to separate your hurts from your heart so you can discern what's yours and what's God's to carry? He has wisdom for you that will bring peace back to your soul once again. He has a path of peace for you that will replenish you before the answer comes. And let's together ask God to intervene in the lives of those you love, in the way only He can.

Consider this your opportunity for physical, emotional, mental, and spiritual reset.

We'll not only replace defeating thoughts with redemptive ones, we'll confront the enemy's attempts to derail us. We'll have an answer for the onslaughts of anxiety, fear, and worry that threaten to swallow us whole. We'll learn to stand more firmly on God's truth even when it doesn't feel true. We'll not only put fear under our feet, we'll learn to believe in our hearts the reason Jesus told us not to fear.

We'll not only revisit those painful memories that surface time and time again, we'll do so under the protection and direction of God's great love and care for us.

We'll not only rid ourselves of some of the destructive habits that have weakened us over time, we'll incorporate some new life-giving habits that will strengthen us and prove themselves in a matter of weeks.

We'll not only identify the roadblocks to our soul-healing, we'll finally have an answer for Jesus when He asks us, "Do you *want* to be well?" Our answer will be a resounding YES! And that's why we're about to take this journey.

We'll revisit John chapter 5 and reconsider the man attached to his mat. We'll take a closer look at his encounter with Jesus and see if we can see ourselves in a similar predicament. We'll deal with the "I can'ts" embedded in our souls. But for now, let's consider a change of heart where we need one. Instead of asking for a break, let's press in and ask for a breakthrough.

> In my distress I prayed to the Lord, and the Lord answered me and set me free.
>
> Psalm 118:5

Consider our time together as an epic journey for the soul. Are you ready? It's time for some spiritual soul healing. But don't be afraid. Focus on the outcome. Remind yourself that when we passionately pursue Jesus and we respond to the inner work that He initiates, we'll be more firmly established in the abundant life He promised us. We'll be strategically positioned and equipped to help countless others find their path of wholeness.

May Jesus pour out His precious Spirit in a fresh new way as you dare to trust Him to live fully and freely through you.

In this with you~

Susie Larson

PS: I am not a doctor. I am not a counselor. I am the poster child for the truth from Scripture that expresses how God chooses foolish things and the weak things of the world to communicate His ways (my paraphrase). This book isn't intended to be a substitute for counseling, nor should you start any diet or exercise program without first talking with your doctor. But if you long to come alive and thrive, I do pray you'll take the next steps with courage and honesty and see if God doesn't meet you in the most personal and profound way.

PPS: I've never written a more raw book. I've emptied my pockets for this one. You're about to get an inside look at my great unearthing. But wow, Jesus met me here! And I believe He's about to do the same for you. This is not a light read, nor is it a book to rush through. Give yourself some time and space to do this inner work. You'll be richer for it. I'll be praying daily for you.

How to Use This Book

You're about to embark on a ten-week journey. I encourage you to look ahead at your calendar and give yourself time and space for rest, prayer, reflection, journaling, and even conversation with those closest to you. You'll benefit greatly if you give yourself a little extra margin in the weeks ahead.

While you'll find space in the book to answer some of the short-ended questions, you'll definitely need a journal or notebook for your personal reflection time, the study questions, and the things that surface for you along the way. If you prefer more journal reflection, feel free to skip the study questions. And if you're more of dig-deeper kind of girl, feel free to pass on the reflection questions. I want this material to meet you right where you live and to tend to the needs closest to your heart.

There's a Spiritual Reset page toward the end of each chapter. We'll pray our way through the acronym PRAISE: Praise, Repent, Ask, Intercede, Stand, and Eternity. This is a powerful exercise and good for the soul.

Also, at the end of each chapter you'll find a decorative page with a word of encouragement just for you. Those pages are also available as free downloadable printables on my website. I think you'll love them.

As things surface for you, dare to ask God for a godly mentor, counselor, or friend with whom you can process your journey. We're definitely not meant to do life alone.

Finally, we've developed a beautiful companion DVD for you that includes ten short sessions, one for each week. Together, the book and DVD set allows study groups to host a ten-week study at home or church, but will also work for those who prefer to work through this material on their own.

One last note—I know this from experience and from the many people I've interviewed on my radio show: It can feel so scary to face past hurts and traumas, and to reckon with current fears and anxieties. Sometimes it feels like they'll swallow us whole. But the enemy is behind that lie. *Jesus allows things to surface so He can set us free.* Refuse to let that enemy bully you into captivity. This is your time to be free. This is your time to walk in a new level of wholeness and health.

Set your face like flint and determine that you will triumph because Jesus says you will.

We're in this together. I'm cheering for you every step of the way.

He Restores

Believe It

Restore to me the joy of your salvation, and make me willing to obey you.

Psalm 51:12

If we will listen with kindness and compassion to our own souls, we will hear the echoes of a hope so precious we can barely put words to it, a wild hope we can hardly bear to embrace. God put it there. He also breathed the corresponding promise into the earth; it is the whisper that keeps coming to us in moments of golden goodness. But of course. "God has planted eternity in the human heart" (Ecclesiastes 3:11). The secret to your unhappiness and the answer to the agony of the earth are one and the same—we are longing for the kingdom of God. We are aching for the restoration of all things.[1]

OUR YOUNGEST SON, JORDAN, used to live on his tippy toes. He walked on his toes, ran fast on his toes, and played football on his toes. He was born with tight heel cords, tight gastrocs (calf muscles), and tight hamstrings. Picture him on the examination table at the doctor's office. When the doctor asked Jordan to straighten his leg, Jordan would extend his leg only to have his upper body drop backwards at an angle. He was so tight that he couldn't sit up straight and extend his leg out straight at the same time. His condition made him a fast runner but would eventually present alignment problems if we didn't deal with it during his younger years.

We helped him stretch twice a day. We reminded him constantly to drop his heels and try to walk on his feet. We massaged the back of his legs and his lower back. Our efforts proved insufficient, and Jordan eventually needed serial casting on each leg. They'd flex his foot a bit and then cast it for weeks at a time. He went through three casts on each leg.

Doctors told us that Jordan would deal with consistent back, hip, and joint pain if he didn't stretch as a way of life. We stretched him as often as we could. But, if you've read any of my past books or heard me speak, you know that Jordan still suffered a serious back injury in high school while playing football. Turns out, the less flexible we are, the greater the risk of injury. (I'd say this is true in life too.)

The ref blew the whistle. The play was over. Still, a player on the opposing team clipped Jordan hard when he wasn't ready for it, and the rest is history. Doctors told us it was one of the worst disc herniations they'd seen.

At one point the doctor told me that the disc blowout severely compressed three sets of nerves in Jordan's spine and, as a result, he could lose control of his bowels at any time. We were heartbroken for him. We heard multiple stories of adult men who ended up disabled from this same injury. This was a nightmare come true for our dear son.

But one day I'd heard two stories of miraculous healings from this exact injury and something rose up within me. Faith, I suppose! I shared the news with Jordan. "Son, you know I've struggled most of my adult life with health issues, and God hasn't miraculously healed me. My recovery has been more of a process. But even so, I believe that He still works miracles today. In the past twenty-four hours, I've heard two stories of how God miraculously healed two men with your same injury. What if we go out on a limb, err on the side of faith, and ask God for a miracle for you? Let's just see what God might do. Are you with me?"

Surprisingly, my dear, reserved son, who'd grown quite depressed from the daily pain and limitations, nodded yes, he was up for it. It's such a beautiful story, I wish I had the space to tell it again here, but suffice to say, one night at youth group, a fellow student prayed for him, and he was instantly healed. A medical miracle.

So few receive this kind of miracle, you'd think this would have changed Jordan's life forever. And it did—physically. Yet he still wandered from the faith after high school. Then the storms hit and God showed him the way home. He was emotionally beat up, bruised, and brokenhearted. And his whole body ached. Especially his back and his hips. In his vulnerable state, he started to doubt that he'd really received a miracle all those years ago.

I grabbed Jordan by the shoulders, stared him straight in the eyes, and said, "Son, there's no disputing what happened to you back then. One day you could barely move, and the next, you were sprinting and lifting weights. God healed you. But do you remember what the doctors told you when you were young? You need to stretch. Jesus will tend to those wounds in your heart, but the physical stuff? I think it's a stewardship issue. *You* have to do that. No one can do it for you."

One day this young adult son of ours walked into our kitchen looking dumbfounded.

"What's on your heart today?" I asked.

He proceeded to tell me that he went to urgent care and saw a random doctor because his knee really bothered him and he needed a brace or support so he wouldn't miss work.

The doctor looked up Jordan's records and somehow a previous MRI showed up (from a different clinic ten years prior). She stared at the screen and breathed out one word: "Wow."

Jordan didn't know what she was looking at, so he waited for her to finish her thought.

She shook her head, looked in his eyes, and said, "That must have been some back surgery you endured. That's one of the worst disc herniations I've ever seen."

His throat caught a little and he replied, "Umm. I didn't end up needing surgery."

Exasperated she said, "No way! There's NO way you're walking today without having had surgery. Is *this* your MRI?"

He verified the information was correct.

Jesus, in no uncertain terms, reminded Jordan that he'd indeed received a miracle back then. And that for this phase of the healing journey, God wanted his cooperation and participation. I'm watching him tend to the things he can and should. And I'm watching him heal from the inside out. He's become the Christ-following man we always dreamed he would be. To me, it's even more marvelous than his sudden-healing moment all those years ago.

Not Much Longer

Recently, John Eldredge joined me on my radio show to talk about his book *All Things New*. We had a fantastic conversation around the whole idea of restoration. I asked him to speak to the person listening who is battle weary and worn out from the fight. He said something like this: "My friend, just tell your soul, '*Not much longer.*' Not much longer. Soon, very soon, Jesus will restore all things to us! There's no loss, heartbreak, sacrifice, or disappointment that God won't redeem many times over. But know this: That redemption process starts now!"

Scripture tells us that even creation groans for that day:

Yet what we suffer now is nothing compared to the glory he will reveal to us later. For all creation is waiting eagerly for that future day when God will reveal who his children really are.

Romans 8:18–19

We'll dig deeper into this passage in the pages ahead, but for now, know that Jesus invites us to expectancy! Right smack dab in the middle of our suffering, Jesus tilts our chin, asks for our trust, and invites us to hope for the impossible. Some of our inheritance we'll see when we see Jesus face-to-face, some of it He entrusts to us now. Today. Can we dare believe that Jesus wants to show us His goodness in the land of the living? Do you think it's possible to experience a radical breakthrough in the body you're in? What about those destructive thoughts that you have on repeat? Can you picture yourself with a thought-life makeover—where once you felt small and self-aware, you now feel larger than life and filled with the Spirit?

God wants to partner with us in our flourishing. He plays a part. And we play a part. And of course, there's another spiritual component to all of this too. We have a very real enemy who aims to do more than just poke fun at us. He wants to steal the precious gifts God has given us, kill any hint of life that springs up from our soil, and destroy any work of God that flows out of our abiding life.

If the devil can't keep our soul (because we've trusted Jesus with our eternity), he'll do whatever he can to distress our soul and to destroy our peace. Thankfully, we're not at the mercy of his whims and schemes. Jesus has equipped us to stop our enemy at every turn.

Jesus wants to help us sort through our story in a way that brings us healing and fullness. He designed our bodies and our souls to thrive. We can trust Him as He leads us through the healing process. And yet there's a measure of wholeness and flourishing we will not know apart from both of these things:

- God's divine intervention *and*
- Our cooperation with Him.

Even if we think we can, we absolutely cannot separate the various aspects of who we are any more than we can separate the trinity of the Father, Son, and Holy Spirit. We are fearfully and wonderfully made, woven together by God's own hand.

Jesus wants us to flourish. He wants us whole. He wants to take what the enemy meant for evil against us and turn it for good. He wants us to live life bold and free, courageous and steadfast.

In order for us to flourish, we need to take the necessary time to examine our most repetitive thoughts and see where they've been leading us.

As painful as it might be, we need to revisit some of the hurts from our past and see if they're still speaking a contrary message to us. We need to better guard our hearts from the toxic influences of the day. And we need to look at our habits and our routines to see what adjustments will bring abundance to our lives so that we can be our best selves. Sometimes the smallest tweaks make the biggest difference.

We also need a few miracles in our lives. How about if we ask for those too?

I'd say the thing in your life that compels you to pray for a miracle is probably the very thing that has taken a significant toll on your soul. Don't lose your sense of expectancy. Dare to hope again. Dare to dream again. Believe that you truly do serve a wonder-working God.

Pursue Healing ~ Pray for a Miracle

Put It into Practice

Focus on . . .

God's Desire to Restore You

Scripture Says . . .

The Eternal is my shepherd, He cares for me always.
He provides me rest in rich, green fields
    beside streams of refreshing water.
    He soothes my fears;
He makes me whole again,
    steering me off worn, hard paths
    to roads where truth and righteousness echo His name.

Psalm 23:1–3 THE VOICE

Do you wonder if Jesus cares for your soul, for your sense of well-being? Read this passage again. He goes before you and prepares places of refreshment for you. He offers nourishment when you most need it. And He Himself is your greatest gift. Spend some time pondering the idea that Jesus *wants* to restore your soul.

Because He really, truly does.

Science Says . . .

Rick Hanson, author of *Hardwiring Happiness*, says, "Staying with a negative experience past the point that's useful is like running laps in Hell: You dig the track a little deeper in your brain each time." But, "*By taking just a few extra seconds to stay with a positive experience—even* the comfort of a single breath—you'll help turn a passing mental state into lasting neural structure."[2]

Pursue Healing

Oftentimes we stay with the memories that take the greatest toll on our souls. Yes, we need to revisit them to uproot them, but those moments need to be reserved for guarded times with godly mentors or wise counselors. The rest of our thoughts should instinctively go to God's goodness and provision all around us and in us. None of us are there yet, but it's a worthy goal. In order to be healthy and whole and for us to notice the Savior's healing work in our lives in ways both great and small, we must *practice* thinking like He does. Our thoughts must flow in rhythm with His.

Does God have negative thoughts on repeat?
Then neither should we.
Does He rehearse how people have hurt and offended Him?
Then neither should we.
Does He constantly condemn and accuse Himself?
Then neither should we.
Does He long for us to live flourishing, abundant lives?
Then we should long for and believe for that reality just as much.

God gives us good gifts to enjoy. And it's actually wonderful for our brains when we engage our senses as we notice all He's given. How good, healthy, and healing it is for you to smell a bouquet of flowers and enjoy the moment, to taste your food and savor it, and to marvel at the beautiful sunset until it brings tears to your eyes. Spend some time this week noticing the good in your present moments, and linger there for a while. It will change you from the inside out.

Pray for a Miracle

Dare to daily pray—out loud so your own ears hear it—this bold prayer:

You are the God who performs miracles, and You're working wonders in me! With all my heart I believe You intend to restore my soul. Open my eyes so I can see You move in my midst. I believe You are doing a NEW thing in me. I want to participate with You in my healing process. May my life be a living, breathing testimony of Your miracle-working power. Awaken fresh life in me!

In Jesus' mighty name I pray. Amen.

Soul Searching

Prayerfully dream for a moment. What would a healed-you look like?

_____

_____

_____

_____

_____

_____

Life Reflection

1. Scripture tells us that the measure we use against others will be used on us (see Matthew 7:2). Part of our own healing process involves resetting our perspective around our suffering and the sufferings of others. Read this passage from 2 Corinthians 5:16–17: "So we have stopped evaluating others from a human point of view. At one time we thought of Christ merely from a human point of view. How differently we know him now! This means that anyone who belongs to Christ has become a new person. The old life is gone; a new life has begun!" No need to write down their names, but spend some time with the Lord and ask Him if you've unfairly judged the suffering of another. Ask Him to forgive you. Ask Him to show you His heart for that person, and even for a glimpse of what life is like for them. Pray for their healing.

2. What we rehearse we remember, and what we remember we live from. What core belief stands in the way of your flourishing? Give some thought to this. If you don't know, ask the Lord

to show you. He will. I had no idea that deep down inside me, I really didn't believe that God wanted me well. I thought He had more important matters to tend to. But the truth is, most of us know that His help for me would not limit His help for you. I needed to wrestle that one to the ground. I now believe—with all my heart—that God wants me to flourish. And I cooperate with Him daily to make the necessary adjustments—be they to my perspective, diet, bedtime, thought life, or whatever—so I can be uniquely positioned to help others flourish too. So what about you? Do you believe God wants you well? Why or why not?

3. Based on what you've studied from the passages of Scripture referenced in this chapter, write out a faith declaration of your own. It might look something like this: *I declare, in the mighty name of Jesus, that God's kingdom is far greater than I can comprehend. And I am a part of that kingdom! I believe God wants me to know His promises and to walk in them, to flourish, to be well, and to help others where life finds them. I've lived too long without expectancy, but now I believe God has more for me. And I am determined to learn from Him, do what He says, and then watch Him do what only He can do. In Jesus' name I pray. Amen.*

Spiritual Reset

"No matter what your situation, for faith to be great, you must believe that God can change your entire situation in one moment with one decision, with one new circumstance. You are to live on the tiptoe of expectation for God to change your life."[3]

PRAISE—Acronym Exercise

P—Praise Him. Write out a prayer of thanksgiving just because He is God.

_____

_____

_____

R—Remember and Repent. Write out a memory of God's faithfulness. Spend time with Him and repent of anything He brings to mind.

_____

_____

_____

A—Ask Him for what's on your heart.

_____

_____

_____

I—Intercede for others.

_____

_____

_____

S—Stand on God's promises. Write out a promise that undergirds what you're asking Him for.

_____

_____

_____

E—Eternity. Put your life, your burdens, and your prayer list up to the lens of eternity. Ask Jesus to help you look up and think long, with eternity in mind.

_____

_____

_____

Digging Deeper

*Use your journal or notebook for this section.

A. Prayerfully read Matthew 9:35–38 and answer these questions: What's the *good news* of the kingdom? And might this good news be more far-reaching than you once thought? Prayerfully ask God to show you something new about this kingdom life to which you are called.

B. Go back and read the passage from Matthew again and consider this: Jesus made sure to address the human condition wherever He went. He touched people, healed them, and consistently spoke truth specific to the need before Him. Imagine yourself walking with Jesus in His day and watching Him minister. Picture a lame man, miraculously healed, leaping and crying and kicking up dust. Imagine a mother sobbing with tears of joy because her child now lives. Write down your thoughts as you ponder His power. Ask Jesus any questions you have. Ask Him for a gift of faith.

C. Hang with me here. Read the passage another time. Picture Jesus' compassion for the crowds. Imagine that look of compassion on His face. Then He turns to you and looks at you with that same compassion. How do you feel about Jesus' expression toward you? How do you suppose He would heal you if you were with Him in His day? Physically? Spiritually? Emotionally? Relationally? What truth do you suppose He'd speak to you? Write down your thoughts.

D. Read John 14:12 and consider this: If Jesus modeled healing, showed compassion, and proclaimed the good news, do you think He envisioned us doing the same but to a lesser degree? It's hard to fathom, but Jesus said we'd do greater things still. What would the increase of His kingdom in and through you look like? Might any limitations lie with us? Do we either consciously or unconsciously limit what God can do in and through us? Are you willing to ask God to answer that question for you? In what ways do you long to see your faith and conviction expand? Faith to see others healed? Compassion for the lost? Conviction to preach truth to those in captivity? Write down your thoughts.

Find the following downloadable print
at SusieLarson.com.

I AM
strong and healthy.

I AM
fearfully and wonderfully made.

I AM
full of life and full of faith.

Jesus is doing a new thing in me!

My Soul and Body Ache

Jesus, Make Me Well

When Jesus saw him and knew he had been ill for a long time, he asked him, "Would you like to get well?"

John 5:6

God's hidden hand is in every event that occurs in your life. In each one His stealth yet purposeful providence is at work.[1]

THIS BATTLE INTIMIDATED AND SCARED ME. And I felt sure that anxiety and fear would swallow me whole. After several painful years battling Lyme disease, and then twenty more years of marginal Lyme symptoms but overall decent health, my life was recently upended by a surge of symptoms that included bone-crushing TMJ headaches and old neurological symptoms that flooded in with new and scarier neurological symptoms. The worst of my physical symptoms raged in my neck, jaw, head, and gut. Inflammation ran amuck throughout my body.

Surges of neck numbing turned into esophageal spasms. Every time I looked down, my neck went numb and if I didn't look up quickly enough, throat spasms made it difficult to swallow. For many months, I got food stuck in my throat about four times a day. Then those spasms moved to my gut, making it difficult to eat more than a few bites of food at a time. Add to the mix surges of anxiety that seemed to come out of nowhere and fatigue that left my battery chronically low.

One morning while getting ready for work, the surges of numbing took over my face, my neck, and my arms. Dizziness spun me around and fear grabbed me by the throat. It seemed like the devil had full and open access to me.

When I first contracted Lyme disease as a young mom, I was still fairly new in my faith. My main symptoms included facial numbing, joint pain, fatigue, and dizziness. Back then I had little faith that I'd make it through that storm. I felt like the enemy had grabbed me by the face and spewed this constant question at me: *Where's your God now, huh?*

Quite honestly, I didn't have an answer for him. But eventually I'd find the answer in Scripture. I fought back with truth-statements like this:

You listen here, devil, NO weapon formed against me will prosper! (Isaiah 54:17). My God WILL come for me and rescue me from every evil attack (2 Timothy 4:18). You will not have the last say in my life—Jesus will! And when He comes, you'll be sorry you ever messed with me!

The more I declared those words out loud, the more my soul believed them and the stronger in faith I grew.

Back then I sensed the Lord promised to heal me. So I contended for full healing. But only for a while. Honestly, when I got *well enough* I left it at that.

Until this most recent storm hit.

Back to that morning in the bathroom when the symptoms raged in me and the anxiety and fear swirled around me. I cried out to the Lord, "Jesus, help me! I can't do this! I don't *want* to do this! Please, Lord, deliver me!" That's when I heard these words in my soul:

The storms reveal the lies we believe and the truths we need.

Read it again:

The storms reveal the lies we believe and the truths we need.

Fear had me by the throat. *What lie do I believe, Lord?* Anxiety surged throughout my body. I felt alone in the battle. Yet standing in that bathroom with panicked breath, I prayed, "Show me the lies that I believe and the truth I need."

Suddenly, I saw through the storm, as clear as day. I identified a lie from the devil that has nipped at my heels my whole life: *I can get to you any time, anywhere. And God will never stop me.*

Thankfully, Jesus whispered to my heart right then, "Susie, it's not true. There *is* a limit to what I'll allow in your life. Someday you'll see not only how richly I've provided for you but also how much I've *prevented* because I love you and I know your limits. I'm not going to let you lose, but I have to let you fight. You've lived your whole life waiting for the other shoe to drop, for the next trauma to happen. It's not good for your heart or your soul to live like that. We don't run from fears; we turn around and face them. Yes, it feels like the enemy has you by the neck, but soon enough your foot will be on his neck [Romans 16:20]. Stand and fight. I promise, you will win this battle."

I began to understand that what happens in our souls happens in our cells. We have to steward our perspective like we steward our health. We have to face our fears or our fears will grab us by the face. If we employ consistent physical disciplines yet live with a toxic soul, we'll still be sick and stressed and live far beneath the flourishing life to which our souls are heir.

What happens in our *soul* happens in our *cells*.

Women (and men too) are battling anxiety, fear, and crazy physical symptoms like never before. One day over lunch, a counselor friend of mine shared this with me: "Susie, we're seeing women in their thirties, forties, fifties, and sixties who have extreme anxiety, fear, and strange physical symptoms. As counselors, we're reminded continually of our tendency to stuff our hurts rather than allowing time and space for them. Well, those things have to *go* somewhere, so they go into our physiology and they eventually get our attention another way. We ache and we hurt because life is hard on us. We need to slow down and make it a priority to sort through our hurts and our fears in light of Jesus' very real and personal love for us."

It's been a little over a year since that day in the bathroom, and I can honestly say I am better for this fight. I know Jesus' love for and commitment to me in a more intimate way than I did before this battle. I have a firmer grip on His promises. I guard my heart with more diligence. I'm determined not to put up with so much from the devil. He fights dirty, but he doesn't have an endless supply of strength. He will wear out if we outlast him. And as much as Satan hates it, Jesus has him on a short leash. He's allowed to go only so far in his attempts to steal, kill, and destroy our lives.

And the best news is this: *Any* battle we endure in faith will pay us back in the end. We'll be richer and wiser for it, and the enemy will have even less access to our souls.

In the midst of my battle, I sensed the Lord's whisper time and time again to reread the story in John chapter 5.

Afterward Jesus returned to Jerusalem for one of the Jewish holy days. Inside the city, near the Sheep Gate, was the pool of Bethesda, with five covered porches. Crowds of sick people—blind, lame, or paralyzed—lay on the porches. One of the men lying there had been sick for thirty-eight years. When Jesus saw him and knew he had been ill for a long time, he asked him, "Would you like to get well?"

"I can't, sir," the sick man said, "for I have no one to put me into the pool when the water bubbles up. Someone else always gets there ahead of me."

Jesus told him, *"Stand up, pick up your mat, and walk!"*

Instantly, the man was healed! He rolled up his sleeping mat and began walking!

vv. 1–9

Honestly, I sighed heavy every time the Lord brought me back to this passage. I instinctively thought, *But Lord, I'm doing everything I know how to do. I get to bed on time. I exercise whenever I have the strength. I drink lots of water, take vitamins, eat clean, take Epsom salt baths, and memorize Scripture. I pray healing verses and ask others to do the same on my behalf. Why do You keep asking me if I want to get well? Of course I want to get well. You have things for me to do in this life; I know this with my whole heart. I'm fighting for a breakthrough. What am I missing?*

Silence. He didn't speak.

He just continued to point me back to this passage. So I changed my strategy.

"Lord," I prayed, "show me the obstacles standing in my way. Show me my own I-can'ts—the destructive things I cannot see but deeply believe." Over the course of the next several weeks, my I-can'ts became painfully evident to me. I had no idea that embedded in my belief system were core beliefs that kept me from completely going after the fullness of God's promises to me.

For instance, before I stepped up to speak one night, I felt weak, dizzy, and very dependent on the Lord. The host whispered to me, "Oh, um. Be sure to tell the women all about your health struggles, otherwise they'll just hate you when they get a look at you." I realized at that moment she was echoing something I've heard before. Women have said, "I'd hate you if you didn't struggle so; you're such a cute little thing." It was always in jest, but their words still wormed their way into my soul. I don't want people to hate me. I've been on the receiving end of jealousy, pettiness, and gossip. It's excruciating.[2]

Right before I went up to speak that night, Jesus whispered in my ear, "Do you want to be well? Even if others revile you? Can you trust Me with your reputation and your heart? And by the way, not all women are that petty—and the ones who are need healing too."

My instinctive reaction was fear. So that lie—that people wouldn't like me if I were healthy—*did* have a hold on me. But I recognized it for what it was and prayed, "Yes, Lord. I trust You with others' opinions, with my health, and with my heart. I *want* to be well." That—for me—was a courageous, faith-filled prayer.

About a week later, while praying for human trafficking victims and the plight of slavery, these words passed through my mind: *Blessing guilt.* Then the Lord whispered to my heart, "*Do you want to get well? Can you deal with healing while others suffer? Do you trust Me enough to work out My purposes in your life and in the lives of those who suffer unimaginably so?"*

This time, my instinctive reaction was nausea. In light of the indescribable suffering in the world, I couldn't fathom asking for more than I already possessed. But I'm sure you know as well as I do that what God does for one does not in any way diminish His ability to help another. And so I prayed, "Yes, Lord, I want to be well. In fact, I want You to deliver me so fully and profoundly that fear no longer has a grip on me. I want to be one of Your conduits to freedom and wholeness. Heal me and heal those girls! Free me and free those girls! Put a fire in my soul to serve you *whole*-heartedly, without reserve, so that countless women may go free."

One by one the Lord gently, lovingly, and truthfully showed me the lies I picked up when life let me down. Jesus' words are still true: *The truth will set you free.*[3]

So how about you? Are you ready to reckon with your own I-can'ts? They're rooted deep inside most everyone, you know. But Jesus wants us free. Listen to these wise words from author Jan Silvious:

> The opposite of resilience is not weakness but "learned helplessness." . . . Notice that the phrase *learned helplessness* is all about what is learned. It is not natural to humans to be helpless, but life experiences can stamp helplessness on our brains. Such an imprint gives a sense of impossibility to a situation.[4]

I remember years ago when the Lord whispered to my heart, *"I'd heal you today, but you'd lose it tomorrow. You don't have the infrastructure for healing. You think like a sick person."* He was right. I've spent the last twenty years renewing my thoughts around health and around what's possible for those who believe. I do think that's why God has given me the grace to live such a full life in spite of a chronic health issue.

Still, my most recent battle opened my eyes to old hurts connected to current fears that needed to be untangled and dismantled in order for me to walk free. How about you?

Pursue Healing ~ Pray for a Miracle
Put It into Practice

Focus on . . .

Your Relationship with Food

Scripture Says . . .

But still, You long to enthrone truth throughout my being; in unseen places deep within me, You show me wisdom.

Psalm 51:6 THE VOICE

The food we eat directly affects how we feel, how we function, and even how we frame our lives. This is a hot topic and I don't want to step on toes here, but I ask you to prayerfully consider what dietary tweaks God might be inviting you to over the next few weeks. I will tell you, I have a family member whose anxiety stopped when she gave up corn. And another whose brain fog completely disappeared when he gave up gluten. And another whose body aches ceased when she eliminated all corn derivatives from her diet. There's not a one-size-fits-all prescription here, but this one thing is true: God is concerned with what we do, and even more so with why we do it. He knows all of our comfort defaults, and He knows when our good intentions are actually not good for us. Even if you think you don't have any issues with food, I dare you to invite God into this aspect of your life. Then follow His lead. He wants to bring truth to the deepest places of your inner being. He *will* show you wisdom.

Science Says . . .

Because they're so intimately connected, doctors and scientists now view the brain and the gut as a single organ. Dr. Anthony Komaroff, a professor at Harvard Medical School, writes: "The brain has a direct effect on the stomach. For example, the very thought of eating can release the stomach's juices before food gets there. This connection goes both ways. A troubled intestine can send signals to the brain, just as a troubled brain can send signals to the gut. Therefore, a person's stomach or intestinal distress can be the cause *or* the product of anxiety, stress, or depression. That's because the brain and the gastrointestinal (GI) system are intimately connected."[5]

Pursue Healing

Given the intimate brain-gut connection, and given that our diet has everything to do with our overall health, here's a challenge—a tough one, for some. But I encourage you to give one of these objectives a try:

- Give up sugar (at least cut way back and see how much better you feel!)
- Give up processed foods (at least cut back)
- Give up gluten (at least start to cut back and get used to life without it; see how you feel)[6]

Pray for a Miracle

Dare to daily pray—out loud so your own ears hear it—this bold prayer:

You are a miracle-working God. Give me a vision for what freedom looks like for me. Give me faith to believe You for my miracle. Show me what makes me tired. Show me what masters me and slows me down. Help me to lose my taste for that which weakens me, and acquire a taste for that which strengthens me. Heal me from the inside out! Help me to make the necessary changes. I want to participate with You in my healing process. Awaken fresh life in me! Amen.

Soul Searching

What ties your gut up in knots? What hurt or fear or sadness sits just beneath the surface for you?

_____

_____

_____

_____

_____

> Lord, You are my precious Shepherd. You care for me always. I lack no good thing. You give me rest when I need it. You restore my soul. You soothe my fears and You make me whole again. I will follow You forever.
>
> Psalm 23:1–3 (paraphrase)[7]

Prayer

Precious Father, I marvel at the way You love me from immaturity to maturity, from brokenness to wholeness. You don't berate me for my blunders or belittle me for my weakness. You meet me in those places and make me strong. You bind up my wounds so they can heal. You give rest to my heart so it can beat strong again. You are with me. You are God Most High. Do a miracle in and through me, Lord! Heal my soul and make me whole. Make me a kingdom-focused woman. Help me to live a life totally disproportionate to who I am.

May others pursue You when they see what You do through me! In Jesus' name I pray. Amen.

Life Reflection

1. Let's go back to a recent memory, one where you felt like your truest self—when you felt safe, joyful, and free. Describe the moment and why it meant so much to you. Close your eyes and picture it. Remember everything about it and feel it down deep. This is actually a wonderful, healing brain exercise. Joy and gratitude around good memories and in the presence of Jesus heal our thought processes like nothing else. Write out that memory and a prayer thanking Jesus for it.

2. Now pause for a moment and ask Jesus to show you the significance of that memory. Jesus wired you uniquely. What gives you joy will be different from what gives me joy. What inspires you is unique to you. And hidden in that fond memory of yours is a metaphor for how Jesus wants to heal, strengthen, and renew you. So ask Him for a fresh understanding and perspective on why that moment was so special to you. Consider it a taste of things to come.

3. Invite Jesus into that memory. Pray something like this: "Jesus, I know that every good gift comes from You and that You made me in a unique and wonderful way. Show me not only the significance of this memory but where You are in it all. If I could see You in the flesh in my memory, what would You be doing? How would You respond to me?" Let the Lord speak to you. Write down any thoughts, word pictures, or insights He provides.

4. Prayerfully read John 5:1–9 again and ask the Lord to show you your own I-can'ts. Be open to His loving correction and direction. Consider what Mark Batterson wrote about this: "If you aren't willing to listen to *everything* God has to say, you eventually won't hear *anything* He has to say. If you want to hear His

comforting voice, you have to listen to His convicting voice. And it's often what we want to hear *least* that we need to hear *most*. Trust me, though, you want to hear what He has to say."[8]

5. Picture Jesus in front of you, the tenderness in His eyes and compassion in His smile. He asks you, "Do you want to get well?" What would you say to Him? Write down your honest answer.

6. Notice that after the paralytic answered Jesus with his I-can'ts, Jesus told him to rise up, take up his mat, and walk. Consider these three directives and ask Jesus what faith and obedience look like for you:

Rise Up: What do you need to rise above (a funky attitude, thoughts of despair, an offense, an old thought pattern, etc.)?

Take Up Your Mat: What crutch or old habit hinders your growth in faith and freedom? Are you willing to lay it down?[9]

Walk: What action do you need to take to partner with God in your wholeness and healing? Is it a physical habit, a spiritual discipline, a shift in perspective? Write it down and ask God for grace and for the *want-to* to make the necessary change.

7. The lame man was healed! The man who lived on a sleeping mat rolled it up and walked free from the circumstances that crippled Him. He'd gotten used to a half-lived life until He met Jesus. Here's a challenging question: Are you asleep when it comes to the active, powerful presence of Jesus in your midst? Are you asleep when it comes to the reality of spiritual activity all around us? Do you want to wake up to all Jesus has for you? Jesus can do this for you too. Do you believe it? Write out the boldest, most daring prayer you have in you.

Spiritual Reset

PRAISE

"Battles are won when we worship. Victory comes when we praise Him!"[10]

PRAISE—Acronym Exercise

P—Praise Him. Write out a prayer of thanksgiving just because He is God.

_____

_____

_____

R—Remember and Repent. Write out a memory of God's faithfulness. Spend time with Him and repent of anything He brings to mind.

_____

_____

_____

A—Ask Him for what's on your heart.

_____

_____

_____

I—Intercede for others.

_____

_____

_____

S—Stand on God's promises. Write out a promise that under-girds what you're asking Him for.

_____

_____

_____

E—Eternity. Put your life, your burdens, and your prayer list up to the lens of eternity. Ask Jesus to help you look up and think long, with eternity in mind.

_____

_____

_____

Digging Deeper

*Use your journal or notebook for this section.

A. As you've worked your way through this chapter, have you identified lies you believe that need to be uprooted? Write them down (even if you've already done so earlier in this chapter). How about excuses? Reasons you don't want to believe God for a miracle? Do you have any of those? Remember, though we can find a thousand excuses on the bottom shelf, we don't need even one of them. We have God's promises hovering overhead, and they're worth contending for.

B. Up to this point, what have those lies cost you? Prayerfully consider the ripple effect of the core beliefs that have held you down. Write down your thoughts.

C. Jesus said that the devil is a liar. When the enemy speaks, he lies, because that's his native language.[11] There's absolutely no truth in him. Picture power lines erected in your front yard. The pole stands taller than your house, and the enemy arrogantly put it there. He uses those power lines to communicate to you whenever he sees an opening. He watches for your body language, your out-loud worries, and your choices. And at the right time, he calls you up and speaks to your heart, mind, and soul with every intention to destroy you and your perspective (in ways both big and small).

I remember a time when I texted my kids on our family text, and none of them replied. Now, what's true is that we love each other and enjoy banter back and forth over text. What's also true is that Kev and I don't see our kids nearly as much as we wished, but they're young adults with busy lives. About a day after I sent that text, I ran into a woman who shared how her adult kids and their spouses come over every Sunday for dinner, and there's no stopping them. They just always want to be together. *Sigh.* Picture the power lines. Her comments tempted me to pull down the lie and make it personal. It felt personal. But it wasn't personal. It was just a fluky day when no one responded to that particular text.

How often do we cause ourselves unnecessary grief because we listen to the lies and fill in the gaps with our own fears and frustrations? We looked at the following passage last chapter, but let's look at it again in light of this analogy: "We demolish arguments and every pretension that sets itself up against the knowledge of God, and we take captive every thought and make it obedient to Christ" (2 Corinthians 10:5 NIV). I needed to pull down the power lines of communication from the enemy and refuse the bait of discouragement, jealousy, or offense. Then I needed to grab ahold of the promises of God and hold on tight because He is very much at work in my family. So what would it look like for you to *demolish* that structure in your front yard? How mad do you have to get to take it down and rip it to shreds? Write out a faith-filled, declarative prayer telling God that you're done letting the enemy rob you blind and distress your soul.

D. Picture yourself cleaning up the mess in your front yard, mowing the lawn, and then erecting a beautiful, rugged cross in that very spot. Picture the love in God's heart and mind for you. Let yourself revel in Jesus' affection and protectiveness of you. Ask the Lord to give you thoughts like His, a heart like His, and a soul at peace and at rest. These are treasures worth protecting.

> **Find the following downloadable print at SusieLarson.com.**

I AM NOT **WHO I WAS.** I AM NOT **WHAT I DO.**

I'm someone God loves and enjoys.

I AM ON MY WAY TO

healing and wholeness.

MIRACLES

are possible for me.

three

I'm Afraid

Jesus, Grant Me Fierce Faith

For God has not given us a spirit of fear, but of power and of love and of a sound mind.

2 Timothy 1:7 NKJV

Living without fear is not believing that nothing fearful will happen but, rather, believing that nothing will happen apart from God's intervening grace. Nothing will happen without the hand of God in control, filtering out what will destroy, softening the full force of the blow, and bringing a result that could not be accomplished any other way. His standard for weighing your situation in the balance before it reaches you is: the glory it will produce outweighs the pain it will cause.[1]

I DIDN'T WANT TO GO TO PRISON.

Yet this thought ran repeatedly through my mind. Fear sprayed what felt like shards of glass into my soul. I felt prickly all over. The undertow of what-ifs about pulled me under. *Where is this coming from?*

I took inventory of my life and found no evidence that I'd be going to prison anytime soon. I followed the law. Paid my taxes. Loved my neighbor. Feared God. You get the idea. Yet this unreasonable fear about strangled me. Granted, it showed up after an intense eighteen-month battle with my health. But this thing seemed to be hitting me out of nowhere.

I fearfully imagined bringing utter shame to my family, friends, and co-workers. I second-guessed the speed limit while I drove. I feared sending an email too quickly to the wrong person. It's crazy-making to think about it now. But fear created a hypersensitivity to my own capacity to mess up, trip up, and fall down (which only exacerbated the opportunity to do more of the same). Without realizing it, I had put more weight on my ability to fall down than on God's ability to hold me up.

Here's where the fear first presented itself in my current-day story: Over the course of a couple of months on my radio show, I'd interviewed several Christian men who'd gone to prison either because they were in the wrong place at the wrong time, or because they'd committed a white-collar crime without realizing it.

With each interview I felt the prickles of anxiety and fear increasingly rise up within me, but I couldn't figure out why. I asked God to speak to my heart and show me what I could not see. He seemed silent while my fears screamed loud. Peace felt like a wet water balloon. I'd have a hold on it, and the next moment—with the next fearful thought—it slipped out of my hands.

Around that same time, people (without knowing my struggle) randomly confessed to me that they were dealing with their own out-of-the-blue unreasonable fears. I knew I wasn't alone. I knew that the enemy was on a tirade. But I had to know if I had given him access in some way.

This much was true: I've battled fear my whole life. It seemed my instinctive response to threat was fear. They say nerves that fire together, wire together. In other words, when we have certain traumatic experiences, we have thoughts and reactions to those experiences, making them one and the same. That's why some of us are so triggerable. Traumatic Experience + Emotion = Perceived Reality and Fear Reaction.

But our God has not given us a spirit of fear (2 Timothy 1:7). Fear is a spirit, and it's not from God. And fear can become an actual habit in our lives. Jennifer Kennedy Dean writes

> We have learned to default to fear. It didn't just happen, but we learned it in such a way that we didn't know we were developing a habit. To rescue us, God promises to do a new thing. To make a new road. The strongly entrenched neural pathway that leads us automatically to fear and worry will be laid waste and a new road (neural pathway) will be created—a road that leads automatically to faith.[2]

> For I am about to do something new.
>   See, I have already begun! Do you not see it?
>   Isaiah 43:19

Physician and author Dr. Timothy Jennings says,

> Our brain has only two motivational fuels: Love and fear. Perfect love casts out fear. When we allow fear to run rampant in our lives, we open the door to a cascade of inflammation in our bodies. Fear significantly affects our health, decision-making ability, and our perspective.[3]

Knowing what I know about fear and its effect on my already challenged health, I went after it with God's help. I couldn't afford to let fear win the day. I wanted to be well. In *every* way. I quoted Scripture, prayed whole passages from the Bible, marched around my living room and took authority over the spirit of fear. I enlisted my friends to pray, and worshiped like I'd never worshiped before.

I cut out TV, Christian suspense novels (my favorite, but they stir me up), and unnecessary food (like excess sugar). I focused my heart and mind on the things of God. I leaned in and appealed to the Lord, *What is going on with me, Lord? Why does it seem the enemy has such access to me?*

Like a weed that sneakily surfaced in my yard, I realized that this fear had its roots in me. Though it felt like Satan had launched another *new* attack on my life, I realized that this current threat was indeed connected to an old fear. Though it seemed like God had done nothing to stop the enemy's threats against me, I realized once again that He has a purpose for everything He does. God is 100 percent committed, 100 percent involved, and 100 percent purposeful in everything He allows into our lives. He only allowed me to be stirred up because He had determined that it was time for me to be free.

In my distress I prayed to the Lord,
and the Lord answered me and set me free.

Psalm 118:5

One morning during my prayer time, a dormant memory played through my mind. One I'd forgotten was there. I watched a movie in my late teens or early twenties that struck terror into my soul. It was a true story about a high school girl who by all accounts was the ideal daughter. She got good grades, followed the rules, respected her parents, and oozed potential. But one night, one of her wilder friends convinced her to sneak out and break curfew.

As I remember it, she hadn't done anything wrong, but the police arrested her alongside her friend, who'd been using drugs and alcohol. Anyway, the girls were brought to the station, and the police officer suggested to the "good" girl's parents that they allow her to spend a night in jail to teach her a lesson. At first the parents were vehemently opposed to the idea. But the officer convinced them that their daughter had too much potential to waste, and that this indeed would scare her into never straying from her path again.

So she spent a night in jail.

But when they came to get her the following day, they couldn't get her out. Because of some fluke with the paperwork, she was stuck in jail for about a month, during which time she was raped and beaten.

I'd completely forgotten about this movie. But at that moment, I physically remembered how it made me feel. All those years ago, I watched that movie and fear *got in me*. If you know my story, though I grew up in a wonderful, large family, I experienced trauma at the hands of some

I'm Afraid

teenage boys. They pinned me down. And another time, another group of teens beat me up.

That movie reflected my worst fears and gave me new things to fear. I was a rule-following girl. A people-pleaser. And yet it *seemed* that I'd lived much of my life without the protections that others enjoy. If this terrible thing could happen to her, it could very well happen to me. Satan, after all, had my number.

I watched that movie as an impressionable young woman and it struck terror into my soul—terror that I didn't know how to uproot back then, so I stuffed it deeper into the recesses of my being.

And I wondered why fear had such a grip on me.

You see how these lies work? I mentioned in the last chapter that for most of my adult life, I believed that the enemy could get to me anytime, anywhere, and that God would never stop him.

But I don't believe that lie anymore.

Layer-by-layer, God has faithfully unearthed and exposed old lies and helped me to replace them with the living, giving truth because He's committed to seeing me free. And He's *just* as committed to your freedom. Isn't that just great news?

It's easy for someone who's not walked in your shoes to flippantly tell you not to fear. It sounds so easy coming from someone else. And many times throughout Scripture we're charged not to fear. But it's not so easy, is it?

Jesus knows the layers of your pain, hurts, and traumas. And He knows exactly how to unearth them without destroying you. He's wonderfully careful with you. And He's ruthless with your enemy. He will in due time heal and restore you. And make no mistake about it: He will also destroy the works of the enemy in your life.

Once I identified the root cause of my current fear, I could face it because it was accessible. It could no longer hide under the lie that God would not protect me. That lie had been exposed and uprooted. Since I was no longer held captive by the lie that the devil could get away with whatever he wanted in my life, I could rise up with faith and courage and refute this fear-threat as well.

The Fear Battle

The devil fights dirty. And life is just plain hard sometimes. Even so, may we stay determined and grab hold of this truth: *God has made promises to us that He intends to keep.*

Let's fight for our freedom so we can know the flourishing Jesus offers us. When we flourish, others flourish as well. Our life, our freedom, matters so very much in the greater kingdom story. We can do this.

Scripture tells us that we have our shield of faith *so* we can extinguish *every* fiery arrow the enemy sends our way.[4] We fight the enemy's lies with the truth from God's Word. Let's look at how my own storm re-

Jesus knows exactly how to unearth the layers of your fears, hurts, and pains without destroying you.

vealed lies that I'd believed and the truths that I'd need in order to walk out my freedom and to know the flourishing that Jesus purchased for me.

- **Lie-Arrow:** I can get to you anytime, anywhere.
  - **Truth-Bomb:** No you can't. Jesus is fiercely committed to me and will only allow you to get away with what will serve me in the end (Isaiah 54:17, Romans 8:28). Either way, you lose, enemy.
- **Lie-Arrow:** You will never be physically healed or free. You will live with constant symptoms that depress you with the unsettling dread that a worse disease awaits you just around the corner.
  - **Truth-Bomb:** I know I will be fully healed and symptom-free. If not in this life, the next. And besides, whatever battle I have to face, I'll face it with the Prince of Peace, and not the spirit of fear (Psalm 103:1–5; 2 Timothy 1:7). Either way, overwhelming victory belongs to me (Romans 8:37) because I belong to Jesus!
- **Lie-Arrow:** You should watch your step because at the right time, I'm going to trip you up and destroy your reputation. You have much to fear.
  - **Truth-Bomb:** You're a liar, devil! God plans to prosper me and not to harm me, to give me a hope and a future (Jeremiah 29:11).

He's the One who is able to keep me from falling and will present me before His glorious presence without fault and with great joy (Jude 24)! Jesus directs my steps. He delights in every detail of my life. When I stumble, I never fall, for the Lord holds me by the hand (Psalm 37:23–24).

In my book/DVD study *Your Beautiful Purpose*, I wrote and spoke about the fear of exposure. Countless people admit to fears of being publicly humiliated or of having old skeletons fall out of the closet for all to see. And still others feel perfectly unqualified to do what they do, even if they *are* qualified and quite successful in what they do. Their greatest fear is that others will see them as the imposter they believe themselves to be. Fear of exposure drives us into hypervigilance, steals the joy from our work, and keeps us from flourishing in our God-given assignment.

> The *closer* we get to exposing and identifying our fears, the more it threatens the enemy's claimed *territory* in our lives.

I've learned over the years that when God allows a storm or a trial, it's a great opportunity to identify our fears so we can grab hold of faith.

The closer we get to exposing and identifying our fears, the more it threatens the enemy's claimed territory in our lives. How does he respond? He turns up the heat on our fears; he threatens exposure and terror because *he's* the one who's terrified at the thought of being exposed. His only power in our lives is the lie. So when the lie goes, so goes his access to us. Hang in there. You will win this battle.

Once you've identified and named your fears, you're halfway there. You've got the upper hand. Fear hides in the dark. The enemy shoots arrows from the shadows into the hidden places in our hearts. That's why the storms in our lives are really so useful to us! And when we grasp God's faithfulness to us in the storm, we'll more bravely face the threats against us.

My husband serves on the board of a ministry that serves the people in Rwanda. At the end of his first trip, the team went on a safari. He came home and said, "I learned something about lions. They have a loud roar and they're fast but only for a distance. They don't have endurance. That's why they rely on their ability to prowl, strategize, and intimidate."

In other words, the fear-lion slinks around in the shadows. He relies on surprise attacks and his loud roar.

> Stay alert! Watch out for your great enemy, the devil. He prowls around like a roaring lion, looking for someone to devour. Stand firm against him, and be strong in your faith. Remember that your family of believers all over the world is going through the same kind of suffering you are.
>
> 1 Peter 5:8–9

The fear-lion prowls around and looks for an opening in our lives, an opportunity to at least disrupt our peace, at worst, to bait us into sin, ruin our lives, and rob us of our influence, perspective, and joy.

> Our fear gives Satan a geographical presence that he doesn't deserve.[5]

The scrawny, emaciated fear-lion finds an opening in our lives where he knows he's already planted fear. He knows us well. He's studied us for years. He remembers well the traps he set for us when we were just children. He knows what lies he fed us when life let us down. He watches our response to certain triggers. And as long as we react to our fears instead of responding to God's promises, the enemy's strategy against us will continually be successful.

The Lion of Judah

One fear I could not seem to overcome in this season was the fear of debilitating disease. Almost thirty years ago, when my neurological symptoms first presented themselves, doctors suggested multiple sclerosis or a brain tumor. I was a young mom, in my twenties with three little children, an empty bank account, and an exhausted husband. I couldn't—for the life of me—comprehend that God was allowing this storm after six months on bed rest due to a high-risk pregnancy.

I'm Afraid

Many of you know the story. I ended up with a Lyme disease diagnosis. And it's been a battle. But the fear of other neurological diseases has nipped at my heels my whole adult life. This recent resurgence of sickness and symptoms became my D-day battle. Time to go to war. Time to put fear under my feet once and for all so I could truly be free.

I pictured myself crawling up on the altar with trembling hands and wobbly knees. I curled up in a ball and surrendered my worst fears. I had to face them, look all the way through them, and see Jesus there. I had to pray the "even if" prayer. "My God will deliver me from this fire, but *even if* He doesn't, He's still my God, and He will ultimately deliver and heal me when it's all said and done."[6]

In that same moment, the Lord gave me a picture of Himself as the Lion of Judah. Picture Aslan in *The Chronicles of Narnia*. His mane flowed in the wind. He was majestic and strong (nothing like the emaciated fear-lion that gnarls at us). I saw Him put one large paw and then the other up on the altar. He leaned over me and let out a fierce roar, from left to right, as if to serve the atmosphere notice that I belonged to Him. This word picture left me breathless in the most beautiful way. The Lord whispered to my heart, *"Right now you feel fragile and vulnerable. But you're only one of those things. You're fragile, but not vulnerable."* I was only fragile. Not vulnerable. I have the living, all-powerful God alive in me, fighting for me, and keeping watch over me. And He's as fiercely protective of you. Praise God.

Pursue Healing ~ Pray for a Miracle
Put It into Practice

Focus on . . .

The Impact of Fear

Scripture Says . . .

For God has not given us a spirit of fear, but of power and of love and of a sound mind.

2 Timothy 1:7 NKJV

When fear attaches to our experience, it's hard to separate the two without intentionally doing so. Since fear is a spirit and it's not from God, it's worth your time to consider your triggers and where they're coming from. Is God big enough to deliver you? Yes, He is! Is He strong enough to defend you? Yes, He is! Is He loving enough to stand with you in your mess and claim you as His own? Absolutely, yes, He is. Ask God to show you where fear is hidden in you. Go after the lie behind the fear and find the Prince of Peace there, waiting to comfort you and to lead you to new places of freedom.

Science Says . . .

Fear is an intruder, an unnatural invader, like a flesh-eating bacteria—ravaging and deforming all creation. Fear impairs our judgment, paralyzes our reason and leads us down the path of selfishness. . . . When fear increases, love, growth, development, and healthy thinking decrease. . . . When the fear center of the brain (amygdala) is activated and is not calmed, it triggers a cascade of caustic events, which ravages our bodies and brains.[7]

Fear costs us in more ways than we know. It's time to be ruthless with our fears so we can lay hold of our freedom.

Pursue Healing

Though we've many legitimate reasons for fear, we can put fear in its proper place. During the worst part of my most recent health battle, I sensed God wanted me to engage in a ZERO tolerance policy regarding fear. Even though my symptoms were scary and the unknown seemed scarier still, I decided to turn my back on fear and give it virtually no room to grow in my life. I decided that if I did have a bigger health battle ahead of me, I wanted to face it with the Prince of Peace and not the spirit of fear!

I'd traveled so often on the pathway of fear that my brain had paved a four-lane superhighway to accommodate my repetitive thought process. But I learned that if I *neglect* that superhighway and I just stop traveling on it, my brain will eventually get rid of it and move on to accommodate my new and most consistent thoughts. It was a fierce battle at first, but eventually fear stopped being my instinctive reaction or my go-to place. For years I struggled with the fear of what-if around my health because of my inconsistent neurological issues. That particular fear is gone. Praise God.

Consider practicing a zero tolerance policy with your fears. When you're tempted to fear, turn your back on your fears and turn your eyes upon Jesus. Ask Him for wisdom and perspective and for a promise to anchor you. Jesus is with you here. He invites you to engage your faith, to know His love, and to find fresh hope again.

Pray for a Miracle

Father in heaven, You are the star-breathing God, and You live in me! I refuse to live in fear because it's not from You. By Your great power, deliver me from this fear! Take away my sense of terror, dread, and angst. Fill those places with hope and expectancy. You are greater than my fears, greater than my circumstances, and even greater than my own tendency to control and self protect. Rise up within me so I can soar with You. Grant me a faith-miracle, Lord! In Your name I pray. Amen.

Soul Searching

What fear continually surfaces for you? Have you ever dealt with an unreasonable fear that seemed to come out of nowhere?[8]

_____

_____

_____

_____

_____

_____

> I prayed to You, Lord, and You answered me! You freed me from all of my fears! I looked to You and now I'm radiant with joy. Shame no longer darkens my face and fear no longer furrows my brow! In my desperation I called to You, and You listened. You saved me from every single one of my trials. They did not destroy me. You've charged an angel as my guard. You surround and defend me because I honor Your name.
>
> Psalm 34:4–7 (paraphrase)

Prayer

Father in heaven, I bless Your name! You are high and lifted up. You are mighty to save! I thank You for Your goodness to me! I'm so grateful for Your commitment to my freedom. Have Your way in me, Lord! Set me free. Completely free! Show me the lies I picked up when life let me down. Show me the ways the enemy has been given *access to steal my life from me. I want to be free. Give me a vision for Your plan and purposes for me. Fill me with faith and courage to lay hold of all You have for me. I want to be a living, breathing testimony of Your grace and wonder-working power. Let's do this, Lord, I want to win this fear-battle. Do a miracle in me. In Jesus' name I pray. Amen.*

Life Reflection

1. The enemy purposely plans and schemes against us. He creates scenarios that seem to come out of nowhere but that are carefully orchestrated to trigger old fears and solidify old lies embedded in our souls. And what do we do? We react. We numb out on our indulgence of choice. We rehearse fearful, anxious thoughts that actually trigger stress hormones in our body. Can you see how specifically the enemy aims to steal, kill, and destroy our well-being by keeping old fears alive? What are your recurrent fears? Can you trace them back to childhood memories? Write down your thoughts.

2. What tends to be your default response to fear?

3. When was the last time you felt a visceral sense of fear? What triggered it?

4. Recurring fears give way to new fears. Most of us have several fears all tangled up together beneath the surface. But we're not too messy or complicated for God! Write out your fears and prayerfully ask the Lord to reveal which one He intends to deliver you from in this season of life.

5. Fear makes us see things that aren't there, imagine things that'll never happen, connect dots and draw conclusions that are absolutely incorrect. Love opens up our hearts to trust our loving Father. Love inspires us to believe the best, not fear the worst. Spend some time pondering the love God has for you. Write down your thoughts.

6. The enemy is a liar, and fear is one of his most consistent tactics. And don't forget, his threat to you is very connected to your threat to him. Let's turn this around for a second. What about your life threatens the enemy? Why is he worried about you being free? What might happen? Dream a little.

Spiritual Reset

PRAISE

"Freedom from fear comes when you remember the reason for the opposition—when you remember that God has allowed it in your life in order to sustain and nurture you. When you choose to face your enemies, it is actually a key to unlocking the provision of God for your life and the lives of those around you."[9]

PRAISE—Acronym Exercise

P—Praise Him. Write out a prayer of thanksgiving just because He is God.

_____

_____

_____

R—Remember and Repent. Write out a memory of God's faithfulness. Spend time with Him and repent of anything He brings to mind.

_____

_____

_____

_____

A—Ask Him for what's on your heart.

_____

_____

_____

I—Intercede for others.

_____

_____

_____

S—Stand on God's promises. Write out a promise that undergirds what you're asking Him for.

_____

_____

_____

E—Eternity. Put your life, your burdens, and your prayer list up to the lens of eternity. Ask Jesus to help you look up and think long, with eternity in mind.

_____

_____

_____

Digging Deeper

*Use your journal or notebook for this section.

A. Read Jeremiah 29:11 and note that these words were for people living in captivity. God called them, through the prophet Jeremiah, to plan for the future in the face of their fears. Note too that the devil doesn't actually know your future. He just knows that God has already been there and left provision for you. Since the devil is afraid of who you could potentially be, he uses what you've been, what you've done, or what's been done to you to bully you into captivity. But God on the other hand? He already knows the plans He has for you, and they're good plans. Your best plans. Dare to look up and over your fears and consider what Promised Land awaits you. Write out your next faith-steps and be sure to take them.

B. Read Isaiah 43:1–3 and consider the scenarios we will face during our pilgrimage on earth. Write out a personal application to each of these trials. For example, what trial in your life felt like you were passing through deep waters? What was your river of difficulty? And how about the refining flames of oppression? Write out the storm connected to these visuals.

C. What were your takeaways from those trials? How are you richer because of them? What do you know about God now that you didn't know then?

D. Read Psalm 34:4–7 and prayerfully work your way through each line of this powerful passage. Imagine if God delivered you from *all* of your fears. Think it's possible? Imagine you—amidst this fear-crazed world—wearing such a countenance of joy that others consistently approached you to ask you what you know.

Look back over your shoulder at the faithfulness of God. Has He delivered you a time or two? And one last thing. You have an angel of the Lord watching over you. Write out a faith-filled prayer thanking God for His faithfulness in your life.

Find the following downloadable print at SusieLarson.com.

I serve a God
WHO TRAINS ME FOR BATTLE.

WHO FIGHTS FOR ME WHEN I'M WEAK.

WHO DELIVERS ME WHEN I'M STUCK.

My soul waits for the Lord.
HE WILL SURELY COME FOR ME.

CHAPTER

four

I Feel Guilty and Ashamed

Jesus, Set Me Free

I prayed to the Lord, and he answered me.
    He freed me from all my fears.
Those who look to him for help will be radiant with joy;
    no shadow of shame will darken their faces.
In my desperation I prayed, and the Lord listened;
    he saved me from all my troubles.

Psalm 34:4–6

A genius God decided to make His home inside you, and when your heart begins to encounter a very real, very present Redeemer in relationship—One who promises to transform and restore you from within—the healing that takes place will naturally produce redeemed thoughts. Your brain cells will then start firing and creating new connections, reshaping the physical structure. Every part of your brain that might be in a deficit because of your past can be repaired and restored by being in relationship with someone who wants to be with you. Jesus wants a relationship with you so badly that He suffered and died to make this a constant reality.[1]

WHY DO I ALWAYS OVER-APOLOGIZE? Even for things that are not my fault? And why is it that when I feel guilty, fall short, or trip up, I consistently see myself on a trial stand in a courtroom, like I'm persistently on trial, always in need of defense?"

My questions perplexed my husband. He shrugged his shoulders and answered, "I don't have the faintest idea." Neither of us did. Kevin is patient and insightful. He's not the berating kind. And I've walked with the Lord a long time. I know Scripture. I enjoy an intimate walk of faith with Jesus.

Even so, the courtroom image remained a regular screenshot in my brain, and sometimes even haunted me. Yet I didn't know why. In the last chapter I described how a series of events stirred up unreasonable fears within me, and when I pursued Jesus in the midst of that season, He, in due time, brought clarity and wisdom to my soul. But in this particular moment, I wasn't there yet.

Over the course of the several weeks that I interviewed a number of former prisoners, I felt sure I was going to trip up somehow in my own life. The threat of messing up hovered over me like a monster licking his chops at the sight of his prey. Where was my freedom? Where was my peace? Why did God seem silent? Again I begged God to show me what in the world was going on in me and around me.

"Coincidentally" during that time, we were working with a financial planner to make sure all of our ducks were in a row. During one of our meetings, our financial guy suggested that we update our life insurance since we hadn't done anything with our policies in about twenty years. He looked at me and said, "You'll both be interviewed on your medical history, and you'll need to get a physical. And Susie, I'm not sure how this will go for you given your more recent health challenges." I nodded in agreement and didn't know what to expect.

One afternoon, a couple hours prior to the opening night of our radio station's writers conference, the life insurance company called for my interview. I had time to spare so I said, "Sure, this is about as good a time as any." Suddenly, the interviewer went into interrogation mode. Now, she was actually just doing her job and was most likely reading from a script, but her voice suddenly felt clipped and straightforward, and I felt on trial as she peppered me with questions: "We'll need your medical records from the past ten years, and we'll need to know about every doctor visit, hospital stay, X-ray, diagnosis, and medication prescribed. Are you prepared to answer these questions?"

I can't explain what happened other than to say that I broke out into a cold sweat. Not because I had anything to hide or even because I was afraid of them denying me coverage. Given my challenging health history, I was absolutely terrified of getting an answer wrong. My unreasonable fears went into high gear. *Will I go to jail if I get this wrong? Lord, I don't want to make a mistake, but what if I do?*

Again, my fears made no sense, but they were visceral for me. And clearly I wasn't prepared for such an extensive interview. But this was about more than just being ill-prepared for an interview. I came as close to a panic attack as I've ever been. I tried to stay calm and asked if we could reschedule this call when I was more prepared to answer ten years' worth of questions.

I put my phone on the kitchen counter, wrapped my arms around my stomach, and bent over like I was about to lose my lunch. I took several deep breaths and whispered a desperate prayer.

"Honey, what's wrong?" Kev asked.

I blinked back my tears and asked, "Do you *have* to have insurance on me? Can't my book royalties be your insurance?"

"Absolutely" he quickly replied. "I don't care about the insurance. But there's more under the surface for you. What's going on? What are you afraid of?" He looked at me with compassion and concern in his eyes. "Something tells me that you have to face this thing. God is up to something here. And so is the devil. But you can win this fear-battle. I know it. You're stronger than you think."

This was one time I didn't agree with my husband. Wherever this fear was coming from, it seemed stronger than me, and I felt sure it would swallow me whole.

Overall, the interview went okay (though I couldn't wait to be done with it). My blood work looked great and, because I live a healthy lifestyle, I actually received a preferred-status rating. Go figure. My fears were more about making a mistake than they were about not qualifying for insurance. But the process sure stirred up my fears.

Facing this interview felt like a Herculean task for me. In my reasonable mind now, I'm embarrassed to admit it. But it's part of my story. And this is how our unearthing works. The enemy keeps things hidden in our souls in a way that impacts us and imprisons us, but also in a way that escapes us. He stays in the shadows and threatens us with our worst fears using information from some of our worst traumas. Yet nothing for the Christ-follower is coincidental or even incidental. God used this time of shaking to unearth some deep-rooted weeds from my soil. Though the enemy threatened to undo me, he was the one undone in the end.

There comes a point when God knows we're strong enough to win the battle. He allows an overplayed enemy attack to position us for freedom. When we finally grasp the lie, we'll recognize our path to freedom. *The storms reveal the lies we believe and the truths we need.*

Unearthing Is Painful Yet Liberating

The following morning, I drove to the writers conference, excited about the full day ahead of me. I reviewed my various roles at the conference: I was scheduled to emcee, serve on a panel discussion, and teach a breakout session. I had worship music on in my car and soaked in the beautiful morning sunshine through the car window.

I prayed for the day and was singing along with the radio when all of a sudden a painful memory surfaced, and I gasped. I put my hand over my mouth and forced back a sob. I couldn't do this now! I had a big job ahead of me that day! *Lord, why now? Help me, Jesus.*

Somehow, by the grace of God, I made it through my morning emcee duties. I tried to relax in the front row as my friend and our keynote speaker, Liz Curtis Higgs, shared about her broken past and her Redeemer who restores all things. She looked out at the crowd of aspiring authors and said, "That thing in your past that you'd rather forget, rather hide? You need to write about that. Don't be afraid to revisit those places with Jesus. He'll be with you. And someone needs to hear your story."

Clearly, God was speaking to me.

The next morning, with my hands wrapped around a fresh cup of coffee and my Bible open in front of me, I let myself revisit the memory that about took me off the road the day prior.

Almost thirty years ago I was on bed rest due to an incompetent cervix (which made this a high-risk pregnancy). This was new territory for me.

One day while in the hospital on an IV in an effort to stop early labor, one of my nurse friends stopped by for a visit. We talked about delivery, doctors, and the process ahead of me.

She looked around, leaned in, and said, "Just pray you don't get 'Dr. Butcher'—that's what we call him." She gave me a penetrating look and continued in a low whisper, "We can look at a patient's incision and guess who her doctor was. He makes the worst incisions, like he's trying to destroy his patients," she said with a shudder. "We've complained about him but to no avail."

I swallowed hard and prayed I wouldn't come face-to-face with Dr. Butcher. Women are never more vulnerable than during childbirth. And what should have been a beautiful—if intense—experience, turned into something nightmares are made of.

I'll spare you the details, but I'm sure you can guess which doctor I ended up with for my labor and delivery. It was a horrific experience. He was angry, rude, and reckless. And after Kev stepped out of the room to call the family, the doctor did a horrible thing while he stitched me up. I've never felt more fearful and degraded at the hands of someone I was supposed to be able to trust, not only with my life but also with the life we were bringing into the world.

When I went in for my six-week checkup with my regular OB (whom I loved), he asked about my experience. The mood suddenly shifted in the room. I surprised us both with my response. I started to tremble and cry, and I couldn't even bring myself to look up at him as the story spilled out of me.

In the silence that followed, my dear doctor asked me to look up at him. I saw the muscles in his jaw flex. I could tell he was angry.

"Susie, I need you to go home and write in detail what you just told me. Don't leave anything out. Get that letter into this office as soon as you can."

It turned out that my doctor knew about similar situations and complaints, and wanted Dr. Butcher out of practice. But that's easier said than done. So I did what he asked. People ask me why I didn't sue this doctor, but I just couldn't. Not only was I reeling from the whole experience, I had a newborn and a toddler to take care of. And my dad was battling cancer. I just wanted to put the whole thing behind me. Furthermore, this incident happened in a day when everybody wanted to sue everybody. People became opportunists and the whole thing nauseated me. Plus, if I never saw the wretched doctor again, I thought I'd be better for it.

After teaching an aerobics class one day—*six years later*—I came home to a voicemail. The local news station said they were investigating a doctor who'd allegedly raped a patient and they'd learned that I'd also issued a complaint against him six years earlier. They wanted to interview me on my experience with this doctor.

Anxiety and fear shot through my body.

Then the machine played the second voicemail, this one from the attorney general's office. They informed me that news outlets might reach out to me but instructed me *not* to talk with any of them. They had subpoenaed my records and needed me to meet them at my doctor's office to get my records and to interview me.

I loved the doctors and nurses at my clinic. My stomach was in knots when I arrived there with a representative from the AG's office. And the thought that other women suffered because I didn't go after him six years prior? Well, I couldn't even bear the thought of it. Talk about guilt.

The AG reps acquired my records and interviewed me. It had been six years since I'd written that letter, and I hadn't seen it since that time. But I didn't need to. I remembered what'd happened. After they interviewed me, they confirmed that my story matched my written letter to a T and that I would make a credible witness. *Witness?*

Can you see where this is going? The American Medical Association conducted an investigation against Dr. Butcher and I had to testify against him. Though I'd hoped to never face him again, I faced him on the stand. I was brave and consistent. His lawyer tried to bully me, and while he didn't get away with it, sitting on the receiving end of an aggressive, accusatory lawyer, I felt like *I* was the one on trial, like I was the guilty one, I was the problem for saying there was a problem. There were several women who testified that day. Doctor Butcher ended up losing his license to practice medicine. But I felt like I'd lost something too. A piece of me never left that courtroom.

Kev and I walked away from the experience that day and never talked about it again. We both stuffed it away and forgot about it for no other reason except we already had a full plate with kids, bills, and life. But you never really forget about traumatic and hurtful events. Your body remembers. Your brain remembers. Your soul remembers. And your enemy remembers. That's why traumatic memories *must* surface—so the enemy's tactics will be exposed. And so God can uproot the weed and plant new seed.

Did you know the body holds on to our experiences? In his book *The Body Keeps the Score*, Dr. Bessel van der Kolk writes

> After trauma the world is experienced with a different nervous system. The survivor's energy now becomes focused on suppressing inner chaos, at the expense of spontaneous involvement in their life. These attempts to maintain control over unbearable physiological reactions can result in a whole range of physical symptoms, including fibromyalgia, chronic fatigue, and other autoimmune diseases. This explains why it is critical for trauma treatment to engage the entire organism, body, mind, and brain.[2]

That's why we need to walk with Jesus through our past and let Him speak to us about what's happened to us and about what we've done, so He can show us that His love is more than powerful enough to redeem and heal every aspect of who we are. When our souls heal, our physiology changes. When our brains start to grasp the Father's love amidst the devil's attempts to destroy us, our perspective changes, our thought process changes, and we are made new.

"It's like these boulders are surfacing in my soil, and like it or not, this is my time to deal with them," I said as Kev and I settled in for a dinner out with my sister and her husband. "Not sure why I used that analogy. It's just what this feels like."

"Susie," my brother-in-law Rich said as he put his forearms on the table and leaned in, "you know that's a thing, right?" He suddenly got a little animated. "Every year, by an act of nature, boulders and stones work their way to the surface. Farmers pay our sons every summer to move those boulders and rocks off of their fields so they can get ready for the harvest. What you're describing as it relates to your soul actually happens in nature's soil."

The next morning at church, I stood during worship with my hands raised high. I felt raw from the unearthing process I was in, but I knew God was in it all with me. Nothing happened by chance. I closed my eyes during worship and thanked Jesus again for His commitment to me. Suddenly I saw the picture of a torn-up field: piles of dirt and stones and weeds. It was a mess. Just like me.

We need to walk with Jesus through our past and let Him speak to us so He can show us that His love is more than powerful enough to redeem and heal every aspect of who we are.

That's when I heard the whisper: *"This fallow ground is hallowed ground, and I've stationed guards around the perimeter to protect you. Those enemy taunts are coming from off of your property, so ignore them."*

My soul is fallow ground? And it's also *hallowed ground*? And plowed up as I might be, I'm completely protected by the One who loves me? If this part of my story was sacred to God—the unveiling of old fears and traumatic memories—it needed to be sacred to me. No more apologizing or minimizing, no more entertaining feelings of inferiority or insecurity just because I happened to be a raw mess. I'm someone God loves, and He was up to something altogether new and beautifully good.

I decided I was all in. I refused to turn back, numb out, or run away in fear. I wanted to wholeheartedly embrace this process of inner healing so I could be fully alive and equipped for all God has purposed for me. *Let's do this, Lord.*

I read up on fallow ground and here's what I learned. When farmers dig up the ground and turn over the soil, they have to let it sit for a while.

Embedded in the piles of dirt are recently uprooted weeds. They still hold moisture and could easily reseed, so they need to sit and dry up so they'll die off. Then the ground can be leveled and prepared for a new harvest.

There are harvests that will grow only once the plow has done its work.[3]

I've noticed three ways that the enemy uses guilt and shame against us:

Trauma—We're not actually guilty, but he gets away with accusing us because we feel guilty and the accusation feels true.

Past sins—We are actually guilty, and if we're in Christ, we're also forgiven, but we may not fully believe that Jesus' sacrifice and victory were enough for us.

Current sins or indulgences—We default to these so as not to feel the hurts that lie beneath the surface; once again, the guilt we feel is real because we *are* guilty. We need to honestly face up to our destructive tendencies; we need to repent and walk away from these things. In due time we'll come to see how they're a poor substitute for the healing power of Jesus.

During a prayer time with a couple of my mentors, the Lord brought up that picture of me being on trial. One of my mentors prayed, "Jesus, show Susie where you are in this picture." I swallowed back the lump in my throat, squeezed my eyes shut, and whispered a prayer: "Speak to me, Lord." In that moment I pictured Him as He walked up to the stand, opened the gate, and took me by the hand. He walked me off of that stand and said to the crowd, "She's not on trial here."

That picture brought tears to my eyes. And a moment later, I saw Him on the stand for any defense I'd ever need. I was no longer on trial.

My overwhelming sense of chronic guilt disappeared.

If you're in a season where unreasonable fears surround you or if you feel hypersensitive about your humanity and imperfections, know this: You will not stay this way. God is with you in it. He is up to something *good*. The devil fights dirty but he will not win. He will not. You will win. So stay the course. We'll get through this together.

Maybe you don't relate to such a drastic battle, at least not yet. But yours is more of a low-grade bout with shame and guilt. It never leaves you, but you've grown accustomed to it. Do you know that underneath that shame and constant sense of not-enough-ness is a place that Jesus wants to heal? Do you want to be free? I pray so. We'll get to deep-rooted guilt and shame in a bit. Hang with me here. In fact, prayerfully read this passage:

There comes a point when God knows we're strong enough to win the battle. He allows an overplayed enemy attack to position us for freedom.

> I prayed to the Lord, and he answered me.
>> He freed me from all my fears.
> Those who look to him for help will be radiant with joy;
>> no shadow of shame will darken their faces.
> In my desperation I prayed, and the Lord listened;
>> he saved me from all my troubles.
>
> Psalm 34:4–6

No matter where life finds you today, this word is for you. Put this book down for a moment and pray through this passage of Scripture again. It's living and breathing. It's powerful and true. Call on God. Ask Him to deliver you from *all* of your fears. Imagine looking to Him with a radiant face, with no shame behind your eyes because you're brand-new, healed and whole. Picture freedom and breathe it in. He intends to deliver you from your troubles, from your painful memories, and even from the unreasonable fears that occasionally surface.

There are things about you that are absolutely precious to God but that you've maybe overlooked, dismissed, or deemed unimportant.

The sooner we start measuring ourselves by God's grace rather than by our past experiences or by man's esteem, the sooner we will be comfortable in our own skin and begin to love our story. When we buy into the lie that we've still more debt to pay, fear and striving will always win the day. We work from a heart at rest because He loved us first.

If we stay the course and trust Jesus in this process, we will more fully grasp the Father's unfathomable love and forgiveness. He will deliver us from shame and guilt and that plaguing sense of not-enough-ness.

When we buy into the lie that we've still more *debt* to pay, fear and striving will always win the day. We work from a heart at *rest* because He loved us first.

And that enemy of our soul? He will lose courage and come trembling from his stronghold. He will lose. And *we* will win freedom and fullness we never thought possible!

Remember, God is more committed to your freedom and wholeness than you are.

You can trust Him. Keep walking. This stuff is hard work, but the payoff is more than worth it in the end. I'm proud of you.

Pursue Healing ~ Pray for a Miracle
Put It into Practice

Focus on . . .

Rerouting Your Thoughts

Scripture Says . . .

With the arrival of Jesus, the Messiah, that fateful dilemma is resolved. Those who enter into Christ's being-here-for-us no longer have to live under a continuous, low-lying black cloud. A new power is in operation. The Spirit of life in Christ, like a strong wind, has magnificently cleared the air, freeing you from a fated lifetime of brutal tyranny at the hands of sin and death.

God went for the jugular when he sent his own Son. He didn't deal with the problem as something remote and unimportant. In his Son, Jesus, he personally took on the human condition, entered the disordered mess of struggling humanity in order to set it right once and for all. The law code, weakened as it always was by fractured human nature, could never have done that.

ROMANS 8:1–4 THE MESSAGE[4]

We cannot fathom the transaction that took place for our identity, our security, and our eternity. But may we spend the rest of our lives pondering the wonder of it all. May the miracle of our salvation never be lost on us; may God's kindness to us *continually* occupy our thoughts.

Science Says . . .

Evidence accumulated in the last three decades indicates that brain cells have a greater capacity for adaptation and regeneration than we previously believed. This characteristic is generally referred to as neuroplasticity. This property of neurons allows for the connection between different domains of the brain, and thereby different functional components such as sensations, images, feelings, thoughts, and bodily actions. . . . Renewal of the mind, therefore, is not just an abstraction. *It means real change in real bodies. . . . The more I practice remembering the things I am emotionally drawn to, the more I become that which I remember.*[5]

Pursue Healing

When you consider the fact that even today we can begin a *new* work in our thoughts, which will directly affect our overall health, why put it off for another day? Start today by pondering, remembering, and rehearsing God's goodness to you and His affection for you. Like me, you may also have some buried trauma that the enemy has used to accuse and threaten you. But as you ponder the Lord's great love, you'll be strategically positioned to face what's buried beneath the surface. Be proactive with your thought life. Ruthlessly *interrupt and redirect* every pattern of thought that . . .

- Steals your joy
- Makes you feel like others barely tolerate you
- Makes you negatively self-aware
- Compels you to rehearse your failures and missteps
- Gives you a pessimistic view of your future

Because here's what's true:

- Jesus doesn't just tolerate you; He's crazy about you!
- You have zero reason for negative self-awareness. You are an heir!

- You are completely and forever forgiven because of Jesus.
- Jesus already knows the plans He has for you, and they're good plans to prosper, not to harm you, to give you a hope and a future. (See Jeremiah 29:11.)

Put every thought through the filter of God's wild and passionate love for you. Practice, practice, practice, and develop new healthy thought patterns that are consistent with God's thoughts toward you. You will experience a miracle transformation in your brain.

Pray for a Miracle

Precious Lord, I know You want this for me. I want this for me. Help me to retrain my thoughts and reframe my perspective. I marvel at how often my thoughts take me downward. But like an eagle that soars in the sky, You call me to set my sights on things above. I need supernatural help with this! Fill me afresh with a strong sense of Your presence and Your peace. Help me to remember the great things You have done. May I one day marvel at how my thoughts reflect a heart and mind that are healed and whole, just like You always intended them to be. Do a miracle in me, Lord. In Your name I pray. Amen.

Soul Searching

What memory feels too big to face? Are you willing to face it now?

_____

_____

_____

_____

_____

_____

Life Reflection

1. We all have embedded dread, guilt, and shame in the soil of our lives—of course, all to different degrees depending on the things we've endured, the things we've done, and the sensitivity of our hearts. How does the enemy use guilt and shame against you? Of what does he constantly accuse you?

2. Looking at your answer, knowing what you now know at this point of your faith journey, would you say that you need healing? Or forgiveness? Or both? Write down your thoughts.

3. Hidden in our souls is guilt for things that weren't our fault but that the devil has successfully blamed us for (until God exposes him for the liar he is). Our constant sense of not-enough-ness is often tied to those kinds of traumatic memories. Once we recognize that our condemner is actually the condemned one, we can receive the healing Jesus offers. Then we engage our faith and trust Him to also be our great Defender. Ask the Lord to bring to the surface any memory that He wants to heal. Wait for Him. Write down what He shows you.

4. Also hidden in our souls is guilt for things we *have* done, sins we've committed but that Jesus has forgiven. There may be memories associated with those times that we've not fully sorted out with God, and because that's so, our memories and our enemy continually accuse us. Thankfully, Jesus constantly intercedes for us. Why does the enemy get to keep accusing you? What about his accusation feels true to you? Read 1 John 1:9 and then read it again. He cleanses us from *all* unrighteousness. Ask the Lord for a fresh understanding of the finality of His forgiveness.

5. When we willfully engage in sin and/or secretly indulge in ways that hold us captive, the enemy has the legal right to accuse us. He's a legalist and will look for every opportunity to take us down. Write out a prayer. Ask God to make you lose your taste for that which weakens you. Humbly repent, and in His strength, rise up and do an about-face. Turn the other way. Start afresh. Picture yourself on the healing path and trust God to keep you there.

Spiritual Reset

"It's because you have battled, because you have scars, because you have suffered that you have something to offer. If you have known shame and experienced freedom from it, there is no one better qualified than you to point others to that freedom."[6]

PRAISE—Acronym Exercise

P—Praise Him. Write out a prayer of thanksgiving just because He is God.

_____

_____

_____

R—Remember and Repent. Write out a memory of God's faithfulness. Spend time with Him and repent of anything He brings to mind.

_____

_____

_____

A—Ask Him for what's on your heart.

_____

_____

_____

I—Intercede for others.

_____

_____

_____

S—Stand on God's promises. Write out a promise that undergirds what you're asking Him for.

_____

_____

_____

E—Eternity. Put your life, your burdens, and your prayer list up to the lens of eternity. Ask Jesus to help you look up and think long, with eternity in mind.

_____

_____

_____

Digging Deeper

*Use your journal or notebook for this section.

A. Read 1 John 5:1–5 and ponder afresh what it means to be a child of God. We believe in Christ. We love Him and we love His children (that includes loving ourselves). We follow in His ways. And we achieve the victory how again? Read the passage and write down your answer.

B. Notice the progression here. First we identify ourselves as belonging to God through our faith in Jesus Christ. As a result of this intimate relationship, we walk in His ways and love what He loves. Then we engage our faith. The enemy looks for an opening to bring accusation. He's either looking for guilt or perceived guilt. Shame and guilt so often come from our literal sin or from our unbelief about the vastness of God's grace. We know when we're sinning and need to deal with it. But how often do we stop in our tracks and refuse the enemy's constant taunts against us when we know that God isn't looking for perfection, He's looking for faith? In which case, we need to fiercely embrace grace. Do you notice a break in this progression in your own life? Do you need to repent or re-engage your faith? Write down your thoughts.

C. Read 1 John 3 (the whole chapter) and consider how important it is to love God, to follow His ways, and to put our hope in Him. This chapter tells us that when we put our hope and expectancy in Christ Jesus, *it purifies us.* Wow. Write down your thoughts and the things that stand out in this chapter of the Bible.

D. Read Hebrews 12:1–3 and prayerfully consider the sins that entangle you as well as the indulgences that weaken you. What are they for you? What have these things cost you? Ask God to show you. Ask Him to give you a heart to take a better path.

> Find the following downloadable print
> at SusieLarson.com.

God uproots the weeds
so He can plant new seeds

GOD IS DOING A NEW THING IN ME!

I WILL SEE HIS GOODNESS IN

the land of the living.

I Feel Anxious and Worried

Jesus, Surround Me with Peace

Don't worry about anything; instead, pray about everything. Tell God what you need, and thank him for all he has done. Then you will experience God's peace, which exceeds anything we can understand. His peace will guard your hearts and minds as you live in Christ Jesus.

Philippians 4:6–7

As we do our part (rejoice in the Lord, pursue a gentle spirit, pray about everything, and cling to gratitude), God does his part. He bestows upon us the peace of God. Note, this is not a peace from God. Our Father gives us the very peace of God. He downloads the tranquility of the throne room into our world, resulting in an inexplicable calm. We should be worried, but we aren't. We should be upset, but we are comforted. The peace of God transcends all logic, scheming, and efforts to explain it.[1]

URING MY RECENT HEALTH UPHEAVAL, anxiety and worry surged within me at the most inopportune times. Granted, I had myself to thank for many of my bouts with these soul disrupters because I managed to worry myself right into a tizzy. But there were other times when I'd be sitting at my table, enjoying my morning coffee and time with the Lord. Worship music whispered in the background while I journaled passages of Scripture that spoke to me.

My heart and thoughts were fixed on Jesus. I'd found peace in my storm. Yet several times, in the midst of those sacred moments, surges of anxiety overtook me in the worst way. One moment my heart felt at rest, full of peace, and the next I felt prickly all over, like the fear-lion pounced from the shadows and roared in my face. I had no defense to prevent it because I never expected it or saw it coming. Those moments made me despair all the more. *Lord, did I miss something here? I'm doing everything I know to do. Help me, please!*

I learned that when you go through a prolonged trial, it may affect your serotonin levels. And when your serotonin level drops, involuntary anxiety surges can increase. So not only was I dealing with my own anxious and worrisome tendencies, I was dealing with my body's involuntary response to the very things that troubled my soul (our losses, my health, and the fear of what worse thing might happen). I felt stuck between a rock and a hard place and had no idea what to do.[2]

One morning, in my desperation, I cried out to the Lord. "Jesus, You promised to give me wisdom when I asked for it. You promised to lavish wisdom on me—more than I need, in fact—when I ask You in faith, knowing that You'll come through for me. So I will not waver in unbelief. I'll wait in expectancy for You to speak to me and give me the strategy to get through this. I know You'll come through for me."

Some days He seemed silent. Other days He dropped breadcrumbs—enough truth to help me take the next step. But one day He laid out a strategy that would carry me through the rest of the battle:

You REST while I work.
You FEAST while I fight.
You WAIT to take flight.

Rest, feast, and wait? My storm compelled me to strive, starve, and strain at the oars. Clearly, there's a way for us to flourish in our storms.

When we allow the Prince of Peace to guard and guide us, the enemy can't touch us.

Rest

During times of stress, chaos, and hardship, our souls get stirred up and our instinctive response is to *do something*. But when the storm in our souls drives us to strive, it's the perfect time to stop so we can more intimately know Jesus in this place.

> Cease striving and know that I am God;
> I will be exalted among the nations, I will be exalted in the earth.
>
> Psalm 46:10 NASB

I love this passage.

We tend to read the words *be still* and *cease striving* as a gentle whisper from God. However, if you read this passage in its context, you'll notice something altogether different. Read Psalm 46 and you'll hear the thundering voice of God roaring loudly above the chaos and confusion of this life.

Sometimes we hear Him in quietness. But sometimes He makes His presence known in power and strength. This is one of those times.

When we strive and strain, we must remember our smallness before God. We must hear His mighty charge to trust Him because *He* is God. We are not. So we can rest. We *must* rest. And when we're restless, we need to get back to our place under the shadow of His wing.[3] Look again at the passage above. The word *cease* translates[4] this way:

- Sink down
- Relax
- Withdraw
- Let drop
- Let go
- Let alone

- Refrain
- Be quiet

The word *know* in this passage translates[5] this way:

- Know
- Learn to know
- Perceive
- Find out and discern
- Recognize
- Admit
- Acknowledge
- Confess
- Know intimately

Think about your top area of angst and anxiety. Is it finances? Does restlessness compel you to get ahead of God and apply for a third job even though He's not asked that of you? Or maybe it's a relationship. Are you tempted to take matters into your own hands and force an outcome before it is time? Maybe it's your health. You've grown accustomed to treating symptoms rather than finding their root cause. Whatever drives you to strive and stirs up anxiety in you, the best balm for your soul is to learn deeper levels of rest even before the matter resolves.

Finding a quiet place to rest, away from the chaos of your storm, allows you to hear God's voice and receive a wisdom and direction that's unique to your situation. By that I mean, make it a daily priority to meet with God and read His Word. Make it a consistent priority to retreat with Him for an extended period of time. Give time and space in your everyday life to ask God for wisdom and then listen for it. Do only what He says. No more. No less. In due time, you'll experience the fruit of the abiding life.

We do much harm to our souls and our circumstances when we race through our stress, trying to avoid dealing with what troubles our soul, or when we decide to force an issue and take matters into our own hands apart from faith. Unless we develop a habit of resting in and trusting in God, we'll develop the habit of rushing and *reacting* to our circumstances. Robert Morgan writes:

> God won't quit on us and we must not quit either. Month by month, year by year, and decade by decade, we can have greater calmness and composure, growing as sturdy as oaks with the passing of seasons. Our anxious nerves can learn to relax in His love, lean on His promises, and trust in His grace.[6]

There's a time to engage and contend for the promises of God, and many of us know how to war on that front. But in the midst of the battle, so few of us know the warfare power of a heart at rest. Jesus modeled this when He slept in a boat that was about to be capsized in the storm.[7] He didn't worry. He didn't panic. He didn't feel an impending sense of doom. He took a nap. And when He got up from His nap, He took authority over the storm.

With regard to your worries and cares, what would it look like for you to cease striving—*to let drop, sink down, relax, and be quiet?* How might you lean away from the thing that stresses you and lean in to the One who holds you? In this very area of stress and strain, imagine what it would be like to experience a deeper intimacy with Jesus, a deeper sense of rest in Him. Can you picture it? What would a more restful, less stressed-out you look like? I pray you'll take some time to get a vision for what God has for you in the way of deeper, soul-restoring rest.

Look again at Psalm 46:10, and discern what obedience would look like for you. Here's a way to personalize this passage:

> *Father, You know what troubles my soul today. But I will trust Your Word. Right now, obedience for me is to take my hands off this thing; to sink down deep into Your love; to let go of my white-knuckle grip; to leave it alone on Your altar; and to be quiet with You for a while. Help me to perceive and discern Your presence here. Help me to distinguish the sharp difference between the enemy threats and Your potent promises. Show me a better way to view my circumstances. Help me to experience You and know You so intimately—especially where I tend to strive and worry and strain—so*

I can more fully know that You really are God. I exalt You over my worries, over my fears, over my circumstances, and over the enemy who seeks to destroy me. You are far greater than all of these, and I am hidden with You. Help me to know You more. In Jesus' matchless name I pray. Amen.

It's important to note that in this context, *resting* may mean a number of things that require initiative on your part:

- A good nap
- Extended time with the Lord
- Worship
- A walk with a friend
- Exercise
- A more consistent bedtime
- Prioritizing that which refreshes your soul and brings peace to your heart

All of these, in increasing measures, became like balm for my soul. During the worst parts of my health struggle I wasn't able to engage in strenuous exercise, but I could go for a brisk walk, and it did more for me than I could've imagined. You may need to upgrade your priority on self-care. But it's not enough to go for a walk or to go to bed on time. Learning when to engage your troubles with a right heart and mind (not a stressed one) and when to let go and entrust your cares to God is a critical part of the process. OB-GYN Dr. Carol Peters-Tanksley joined me on my radio show to talk about the physical and spiritual implications of fear and anxiety. In her book *Overcoming Fear and Anxiety Through Spiritual Warfare*, she wrote

Instead of eliminating stress, your goal should be to make stress work for you rather than against you. Unmanaged stress is a huge source of fear and anxiety. As with your physical health and your thinking, you need to learn how to take charge of your stress. You will be able to manage a lot more stress than you ever thought possible if you remember two things: you always have more choices than you think, and your "stress muscles" will strengthen as you *alternate* periods of exertion with periods of rest. . . . Out loud, place your worries, fears, stress, or anxiety in God's hands, and ask Him to give you rest. You can know that He will be caring for you even as you sleep.[8]

This is a challenge for each and every one of us. Rest is an act of faith. It can also be an act of war against the enemy of your soul. Do you know what happens when we take our hands off of our cares and entrust them to a living, loving, all-powerful God? He intervenes in the most magnificent ways! Picture Jesus with that smile that goes all the way up to His eyes (this is my favorite way to picture Him). Imagine the sparkle in His eyes as He puts His scarred hands on your face, and with full assurance and joy He says to you, "My dear one, I *want* you to rest while I work. It makes my heart sing when you trust Me. So rest those restless parts of you and see what I—in My love and wisdom—will do for you."

> Rest is an act of *faith*. It can also be an act of war against the enemy of your *soul*.

Jesus Himself said these words to His disciples, and they were meant for us too:

> Peace I leave with you. My peace I give to you. I do not give to you as the world gives. Your heart must not be troubled or fearful.
>
> John 14:27 HCSB

Picture Jesus in front of you again, this time urging you not to let your heart be troubled or fearful. The word *troubled* translates this way:[9]

- To cause inward commotion
- To agitate (by the movements of its parts to and fro)
- To strike one's spirit with fear and dread
- To perplex the mind of one by suggesting scruples or doubts

Review this list and consider how easily we are stirred, agitated, and perplexed. Why is that? My guess in part is that we have an enemy that's studied us for many years and knows exactly how to agitate us into a place of distress and double-mindedness. And then there's the condition of our souls; we've allowed unresolved hurts, fears, and disappointments to fester beneath the surface. We race through our days. We push down the stuff that surfaces and we numb the moment with faux comforts so we don't have to feel what's really troubling us inside. But eventually Jesus wants to bring these things to the surface so He can show us how to access His peace and rest when we need it most.

If you find yourself more easily agitated these days, or if your soul is in a state of unrest, perhaps it's time to come away for a while and find a new sense of rest in Your Savior, who's been waiting for you.

> Let the peace of Christ [the inner calm of one who walks daily with Him] be the controlling factor in your hearts [deciding and settling questions that arise]. To this peace indeed you were called as members in one body [of believers]. And be thankful [to God always].
>
> Colossians 3:15 AMP

Feast

When you're tempted to strive, it's time to rest. When you're taunted by the enemy's threats, it's time to feast.

In the medieval times, armies would feast before heading out to war, both to raise spirits and to store up strength because they most likely wouldn't eat well while fighting. They knew this might be their last meal with friends and family. How much more powerful is it that Jesus *prepares the feast for us on the battlefield*! And why? To raise our spirits and to give us rest. Not because it's our last meal, but because it's His way of making sure we are filled with what we need to win a sound victory. We are not malnourished soldiers fighting for our lives; we are royal heirs watching our enemy be defeated.[10]

> You prepare a table before me in the presence of my enemies.
> You have anointed and refreshed my head with oil;
> My cup overflows.
>
> Psalm 23:5 AMP

In Christ Jesus, we have a place at the Table of Grace. He's made us heirs of God, joint heirs with Him.[11] When the enemy of our soul seeks to steal, kill, and destroy us, it's in that very place, on that very battlefield, that Jesus puts on a feast. He sets up a royal table and furnishes us with everything we need and then some. The word *table* in this verse translates[12] this way:

- King's table
- For private use
- For sacred use

Imagine that! Right in front of the enemy of our souls, right in the face of his scowls and taunts, Jesus lays out a *royal* feast for us. This isn't a tossed-together picnic. It's a battlefield feast—a table flourishing with nourishment and provision.

For me, this feast looks like fresh words from Scripture jumping off the page during moments of reflection, worship songs that usher me right into the Lord's gates with a heart of gratitude, an unexpected text from a friend with a timely word of hope, a special dinner date with our kids where we laugh until our faces hurt, a bike ride by the lake, where I'm reminded of God's goodness, and the right book at the right time that helps reframe my perspective.

Jesus sets your table with what you need when you need it. Look around and notice how He provides for you. Taste and see that the Lord is good.

Imagine Jesus with eyes of steel looking square at His enemy as He provides for *you* on the battlefield. He picks up a chalice and pours anointing oil on your head as a sign that you are set apart and fully equipped to make this journey and to emerge from your battles stronger, wiser, and more discerning. Every single time.

Jesus prepares a kingly table and anoints us with His power and authority, and in doing so serves the enemy notice (and reminds us) that we belong to the King of kings. We are citizens of a great and mighty kingdom, one that the gates of hell will never overtake or defeat. We are part of the conquering army of God.

Once I grasped the significance of the Table of Grace and Jesus' willingness to meet me on the battlefield, I decided to take Him up on it.

When the enemy taunted me with fears, what-ifs, and imagined terrors, I'd picture myself at the table. And this may or may not work for you, but I'd have communion right in my own home. I'd lift up the bread and remember that Jesus was broken for me so that I could be made whole. Then I'd lift up my grape juice, hold it up, and remember the price Jesus paid for my salvation and freedom and the victory He won for me there. Amazingly, in that place of access and remembrance, my worries and fears seemed trite in the face of His glory and grace.

But this isn't just about communion. There's something sacredly beautiful about breaking bread with fellow Christ-followers. I know that—especially amidst certain storms—the thought of having people over sounds downright daunting. But even during such times, a meal around *someone's* table can be more important than we know. What if we slowed down long enough to consider our mealtimes with family and friends a reminder of God's promise to provide for, deliver, and defend us?

Just as rest is an act of faith, feasting at the table can be an act of war—a reminder to the enemy that we will continue to partake of the Lord's provision until He comes again. We will laugh, enjoy, and delight in the Lord, even through the most trying seasons of life. We can and we will feast at His table on our battlefields because Jesus knows how much we need reminders of *all* that we possess in Him.

We tend to isolate when we're anxious and worried. Maybe it's time to plan a party.

Trevin Wax writes

Happiness is contagious. Easter morning overtakes Good Friday's mourning. Whenever we eat together, we put a stake in the ground and make a declaration: *The Lord of the resurrection is the Lord of the resurrection feast.* When we gather, we demonstrate our faith that resurrection life will overcome death, that good will ultimately triumph over evil, that all of this world's heartache is merely "the storm before the calm," as Andrew Peterson sings. . . . So draw up your battle lines . . . gather around this table, raise a toast to the King and the coming kingdom, and fight back.[13]

Wait to Take Flight

My health relapse lasted over two years. And just when I thought my season of replenishment was upon me, I had a relational conflict that blindsided me. Hit me out of nowhere. I was already battle-weary; I couldn't believe God allowed the enemy to shoot an arrow so close to home. Have you ever been there? Have you walked through a long, drawn-out war, sensed your breakthrough was on the horizon, only to step on a landmine?

David and his mighty men returned from the battlefield weary, worn out, and ready to reunite with their families. But when they returned home, they were undone by what they saw.

> Three days later, when David and his men arrived home at their town of Ziklag, they found that the Amalekites had made a raid into the Negev and Ziklag; they had crushed Ziklag and burned it to the ground. They had carried off the women and children and everyone else but without killing anyone.
>
> When David and his men saw the ruins and realized what had happened to their families, they wept until they could weep no more.
>
> 1 Samuel 30:1–4

They wept until they could weep no more. Hard to fathom their devastation. Already exhausted from the battle, David and his men stood on the edges of their hometown only to find ruins, ashes, and loss. To make matters worse, David's men—in their traumatized state—turned on David and threatened to stone him. Let's read what happened next:

> David was now in great danger because all his men were very bitter about losing their sons and daughters, and they began to talk of stoning him. But David found strength in the Lord his God.
>
> 1 Samuel 30:6

Their souls were grieved. Their hearts were broken. On top of it all, David's closest confidants turned on him. It was like the enemy dropped a bomb in the heart of all David loved and cared about. What did David do in his weary, fragile state? *He strengthened himself in the Lord.* What did that look like for him? My guess is that he reminded his soul what was true about God. He remembered his history with God. He recited the promises of God. Maybe he even sang a song or two like he did when he was a shepherd boy.

Interestingly enough, this low, low point for David *preceded his promotion.* A couple chapters later we read that David was anointed king of Judah.

Don't you think it's interesting that just prior to David's promotion, he endured a trial that struck him deep in the center of his soul? How often the enemy strikes hardest just before we're about to break through. We double over in despair, barely able to catch our breath. And during such times, we feel pretty sure that God has looked away or forgotten about us.

Has this happened to you? Maybe the enemy shot a fiery arrow right into the heart of your marriage, or at your children or a close relationship. Nothing makes us lose heart faster than a conflict or heartbreak close to home. When the enemy is allowed to get away with what he does, we cannot fathom that God is carefully watching the battle, orchestrating circumstances for His glory and for our benefit. But He is and will continue to do so.

There were times that I felt the long battle down in my bones. It had become a part of me. Instead of recounting God's promises, I recounted how many hours, days, and years I'd been fighting this battle, and it caused me despair, which made me especially susceptible to anxiety. But when I looked up and strengthened myself in the Lord, I found new strength, new courage to take a few more steps. And though He promises grace for each moment, He also promises increase to those who wait on Him.

God is actively involved in our lives so we can hold on to the promise that after we have suffered awhile, He Himself will rescue, restore, and establish us.

In his kindness God called you to share in his eternal glory by means of Christ Jesus. So after you have suffered a little while, he will restore, support, and strengthen you, and he will place you on a firm foundation.

1 Peter 5:10

When you're tempted to strive, it's time to *rest*. When you're taunted by the enemy's threats, it's time to *feast*. When you feel defeated and you've lost your motivation in battle, it's time to *wait on the Lord*, expectantly believing that He will renew your strength. His word is true. It's impossible for Him to fail you.

> Have you never heard?
>> Have you never understood?
> The Lord is the everlasting God,
>> the Creator of all the earth.
> He never grows weak or weary.
>> No one can measure the depths of his understanding.
> He gives power to the weak
>> and strength to the powerless.
> Even youths will become weak and tired,
>> and young men will fall in exhaustion.
> But those who trust in the Lord will find new strength.
>> They will soar high on wings like eagles.
> They will run and not grow weary.
>> They will walk and not faint.
>>>> Isaiah 40:28–31

The word *wait* in this passage also means to trust in the Lord, and it translates this way:[14]

- Look for
- Hope
- Expect
- Eagerly wait for
- Linger for

Has God made certain promises to you? How long has it been since you reviewed them, prayed through them, and stood in faith because of them? And if you're someone who answers no to those questions, I invite you— better yet, Jesus invites you—to search the Scriptures for a promise that speaks to your problem. Talk to Him about it. Pray the passage. And dare to trust that God's Word is true for you.

We all become battle-weary. We need fresh strength, new zeal, and the otherworldly power Jesus promised us. How do we receive such gifts? We position ourselves on the path of His promises. In other words, we reengage our faith, we reset our gaze, we tell ourselves the redemptive truth—that it's impossible for God to fail us. And then, we wait on Him.

Maybe it's time to linger in God's presence, to lean in and eagerly wait for Him. Ask God for a fresh vision for your next place of promise. Ask Him to show you what *new* power and *new* strength would look like in you and through you. Identify more with His promises than you do with your problems. And if you've gone too long without seeing the sun, determine to remember that your days in glory will far exceed your days of trouble. Today would be a great day to tell your soul to trust in the name of Jesus, because He will most certainly come for you!

> The Spirit is calling us to dance with him into the war zone, fully armed and prepared to destroy the enemy with grace, with spiritual power.[15]

Pursue Healing ~ Pray for a Miracle
Put It into Practice

Focus on . . .

Overcoming Anxiety

Scripture Says . . .

I pray that your hearts will be flooded with light so that you can understand the confident hope he has given to those he called—his holy people who are his rich and glorious inheritance.

Ephesians 1:18

Science Says . . .

If you have a genetic predisposition to fear and anxiety, you may have to work harder than others at overcoming them, but you can still do so.[16]

By removing debilitating self-judgment and critique, a mind can more readily and easily adapt to positive change and results. Our minds thrive under freedom.[17]

Pursue Healing

If you struggle with occasional bouts of anxiety, talk with your doctor. But in the meantime, here are a few suggestions that may help alleviate some of your physiological stress:

- Exercise consistently. (Push yourself a bit; get your heart rate up, and give yourself plenty of time to cool down.)
- Drink lots of water.
- Practice regular deep-breathing exercises. (Here's one: Breathe in slowly for eight counts, hold your breath for eight counts, then release slowly, for sixteen counts.) This is a great exercise for just before bedtime too. Repeat the cycle until you fall asleep.
- Refuse thoughts of self-contempt; instead, practice self-compassion.
- Pray the Scripture out loud. Personalize and declare to your own soul who you are and what you possess.
- Refuse to catastrophize.
- Refuse to worry about what others might think of you.
- Worship as often as you can.
- Once again, consider reducing your sugar, corn, and gluten intake.
- Put something on your calendar that you're excited about (it's interesting how excitement and anxiety are so closely related, but one is good for you and the other is not). It's good for you to have something to look forward to.

Pray for a Miracle

Lord Jesus, here I am again, asking You to do what only You can do in my life. Scripture tells me that You are the same yesterday, today, and forever. You are the God who performs miracles! So do a miracle in me! Deliver me from my tendency toward anxiety and worry. Show me how You fight for me. Give me a vision for what a healthy, healed me looks like, and help me to go after that woman with tenacity and purpose. Take my efforts and multiply them, Lord. My soul waits for You to do what only You can do. I love You, Lord. Amen.

Soul Searching

What steps do you need to take to move away from anxiety and toward the peace of God (time with the Lord, a good nap, exercise, time with friends, etc.)?

_____

_____

_____

_____

_____

> I refuse to worry about anything. I will, instead, pray about everything. I'll take every chance I get to tell God what I need, and I won't forget to thank him for all He has done. God promises me that as I trust Him, I will experience His peace in increasing measures. His peace is profound and unfathomable and exceeds anything I can understand; still, it's mine, and so I trust Him. As I turn my back on worry and turn my heart toward Jesus, His peace will guard my heart and mind as I live in Christ Jesus.
>
> Philippians 4:6–7 (paraphrase)

Prayer

Father, I ask You for a fresh vision for what breakthrough will look like in my life. Help me to pursue healing while I wait for my miracle. Show me how to rest right in the middle of the storm. Help me to enjoy the feast You prepare for me, right in the middle of the battlefield. I want my whole life to testify that there's a God in heaven who knows my name and who will get me safely home. Fill me afresh with the wonder of Your love and power. I am determined to win this battle with anxiety. Help me to discern when to rest, when to feast, and how to actively engage my faith as I wait for You to break through. May my life display Your power. Do the impossible in and through me, I pray. Amen.

Life Reflection

1. Sometimes we find ourselves stirred up, full of anxiety. Other times we're past that point and feel mostly exhausted from battle and just sad. Whether you're in one of these seasons or not, write out the sources of your own anxiety (kids, finances, marriage, friendships, etc.).

2. Linger with God around your answer to the previous question. What lies beneath the angst for you? Is it fear? Lack of control? Lack of trust? As best you can, identify the issue and write it out.

3. Consider the strategy mentioned earlier in the chapter: *You rest while I work. You feast while I fight. You wait to take flight.* Which of these comes naturally to you? Which of these feels less natural? Are you willing to engage with God anyway and see if He'll meet you there? Write down your thoughts.

4. Scripture says that God works for those who wait for Him (Isaiah 64:4); God fights for us (Exodus 14:14; Psalm 18); and He renews our strength (Psalm 23; Isaiah 40). What do you need most from God right now? Write out a prayer to Him.

5. Are you actively waiting on God for the desires of your heart? Are you leaning in and listening for that still, small voice? Do you have a sense of what breakthrough would look like for you? Write down your thoughts.

Spiritual Reset

┌─ **PRAISE** ─────────────────────────────────────┐
│ Think honestly and specifically about those things that │
│ cause you the most frequent and intense periods of │
│ anxiety. Now bring all those things under the authority of │
│ God's Word.[18] │
└──┘

PRAISE—Acronym Exercise

P—Praise Him. Write out a prayer of thanksgiving just because He is God.

_____

_____

_____

R—Remember and Repent. Write out a memory of God's faithfulness. Spend time with Him and repent of anything He brings to mind.

_____

_____

_____

A—Ask Him for what's on your heart.

_____

_____

_____

I—Intercede for others.

_____

_____

_____

S—Stand on God's promises. Write out a promise that under-girds what you're asking Him for.

_____

_____

_____

E—Eternity. Put your life, your burdens, and your prayer list up to the lens of eternity. Ask Jesus to help you look up and think long, with eternity in mind.

_____

_____

_____

Digging Deeper

*Use your journal or notebook for this section.

A. Read Isaiah 41:10 NIV and notice that *fear* speaks of unrest over what might happen, whereas *dismay* describes unrest over something that has already happened. Yet God tells us to turn away from both of these things. We instinctively react to unsettling circumstances, but we're not meant to stay unsettled. Look again at the verse and write out God's reason for calling you to stand strong when you're tempted to be agitated.

B. Read Psalm 62:1–2, 5–8 and consider this: If we can trust Him with our eternity, we can trust Him with whatever threatens to disrupt our peace. Look at the metaphors used to describe God (rock, fortress, refuge). We're actually sturdier in Him than we realize. Picture yourself in a secure fortress where no enemy can reach you. Spend some time praying through these verses and ask God to bring a right perspective to your current circumstances. Write out a prayer declaring God's protection and direction in your life.

C. Read Zephaniah 3:17 (the NLT translation, if possible). Go back for a moment to the strategy the Lord gave me amidst my battle: *You rest while I work. You feast while I fight. You wait to take flight.* Look again at this passage from Zephaniah. Picture Him on the battlefield with you, singing over you, rejoicing in who He's made you to be. Write out a prayer thanking Him for His presence on your battlefield.

D. Read Joshua 1:9 and tell your soul, "Be strong and courageous! The Lord is with you wherever you go!" Something happens in our soul and in our cells when we declare God's Word over our lives. When I tell my soul, "Be strong and courageous!" I feel different. And I know that God never asks me to do anything that He won't also equip me to do. Write out a bold faith declaration, one that you'll speak to your soul in the days ahead.

> **Find the following downloadable print at SusieLarson.com.**

I WILL **REST** WHILE GOD WORKS.

I WILL **FEAST** WHILE HE FIGHTS.

I WILL **WAIT** TO TAKE FLIGHT.

GOD CAN ACCOMPLISH MORE

in a moment

THAN I CAN IN A THOUSAND LIFETIMES.

MY BATTLE STRATEGY IS
TO TRUST HIM MORE.

He's a wonder-working God.

six

I'm Grieving

Jesus, Heal My Heart

You have turned my mourning into joyful dancing.
> You have taken away my clothes of mourning and clothed
> > me with joy,
that I might sing praises to you and not be silent.
> O Lord my God, I will give you thanks forever!

Psalm 30:11–12

Our pain matters. It matters to God, and it matters to us. Yet we can be tempted to manage our pain by minimizing it. We convince ourselves, *I can handle it. I'm fine. It will go away eventually. . . .* But when you minimize your pain, you actually give it more power. Sweet sister, ignoring pain is not strength. It leads to greater injury. Though our bodies have been exquisitely designed, our wounds need attention and care.[1]

WHEN DR. TROY PRESSED ON MY STOMACH, I groaned in pain. "You have lots of inflammation in your body right now. And all of your scar tissue hinders the healing process." My mind drifted back to a time just weeks after my husband's cancer surgery. The nurses instructed us to use this little device on Kev's belly to break down the scar tissue so we could keep it at a minimum.

Scar tissue is dry and brittle. It causes normally slippery organs that glide smoothly to get hooked up or stick together. This can cause pain and even obstruction in our body.

Hmmm. Scar tissue. This was something God wanted me to ponder.

Two days later I met a friend for lunch. I couldn't wait to see her. She's brilliant and deep, sincere and thoughtful. And what a story! From my vantage point, God is just getting started with her.

My friend battled infertility for seven years. Absolutely heartbroken, she and her husband tried their best to navigate life without children. Every baby shower, every Sunday sermon about families, and every mom pushing her little one in a stroller reminded my friend of that ache in her heart and the barrenness of her womb. Deep soul wounds from childhood sexual abuse only added to her sense of loss and heartbreak. She looked around at others who flourished where she only lacked and couldn't help but wonder why God hadn't answered her prayer.

My friend shared this with me:

For me, some of the most painful times were when I learned that my friends were having children—that our kids would never be the same age or have playdates or go through life together. Mother's Day was SUPER hard, as were holidays in general. One Christmas in particular was incredibly painful—hard to celebrate the birth of a baby when yet another treatment failed to work.

For years she considered in vitro fertilization but feared the pre-procedure exam. She knew there was a chance they'd tell her that in vitro wouldn't work for her. She avoided this test because she just couldn't bear the finality of it all. Secretly, she believed their infertility was all her fault—that she was flawed and defective and was somehow to blame for their barrenness. So to move ahead with this procedure only to have it fail meant not only that there would be virtually no earthly chance of her getting pregnant, but also that her fears and assumptions about herself might be true.

She pursued counseling to sort through the painful core beliefs swirling around in her soul. And—thank you, Jesus—she experienced significant emotional healing and spiritual breakthrough as a result. After some deep inner work, she decided she *was* ready to see if she could be a candidate for the procedure. Prior to this, the doctors could find nothing wrong with my friend or her husband. They had no idea why she couldn't get pregnant.

The day arrived. The doctor used a scope to get a look at the uterus, but as they started the procedure, they couldn't get past the cervix because it was completely blocked, covered with a significant amount of scar tissue from the trauma she'd experienced as a child.

Her doctor was shocked. She told my friend, "Hold on, I'm going to keep going. I'm going to push through this scar tissue and see if we can get to the other side." Without any medication to numb the pain, my friend braced herself, and after a few painful jabs, the doctor finally broke through. She removed the remaining scar tissue, and once she got to the other side, she saw a viable, healthy uterus, a perfect atmosphere for new life to grow and flourish.

"How was that for you?" I asked her, just weeks after that experience.

"One of the most painful things I've ever endured," she replied. "But I am learning that when you work *with* the pain and not against it, healing and breakthrough can come."

After the procedure, the doctor looked at my friend with tender eyes and said, "I'm so sorry. I know that was painful, but I think we may have just found the reason you couldn't get pregnant. In fact, I wouldn't be surprised to see you back here in a month to let me know that you *are* pregnant!"

And that's exactly what happened.

I cry just thinking about it. There's SO much more to this story, I wish I had time to share it all. But I will say, even before she got pregnant, she and her husband sensed the winds of change starting to blow. They sought God for direction. They sold their house, left successful careers, and moved away from friends, family, and community. They felt called by

God to purchase some land out of town and start a retreat center. They took a number of faith risks, and God met them every step of the way.

I sat with my friend at lunch that day and watched her rub her belly—pregnant with baby number *two*. She recounted her story with such awe and wonder. It was almost more than I could handle. They went from feeling helpless, broken in their land of barrenness, to seeing their dreams come true as God led them to a place of fruitfulness.

Think about this for a moment: It was several thick layers of scar tissue—from past trauma—that blocked their progress. I can't help but wonder how often our past hurts stand in the way of our future promised land.

The morning after I caught up with my amazing friend, I wrote this in my journal:

I can now look back and see that this actually has been a year of major breakthrough for me. I've broken through, by God's grace, years of scar tissue that has blocked my progress for far too long. And what a painful yet necessary process it has been. I see now that in order for my life to be compatible with new life and new levels of fruitfulness, I need to break through. I'm still breaking through. There's more in me that needs the scalpel. Jesus, have Your way in me. Help me to trust in You. I marvel at Your commitment to me. Glorify Your name. Amen.

For some reason I had this idea that breakthrough would be like winning a lottery ticket. You wake up one day and you get the call, or the letter, or you turn a sudden corner and your life changes forever. And while those all-of-a-sudden moments are often a part of the process, we can't ignore the pain that almost always precedes the promise. I'd say that more often than not, breakthrough is messy and painful and even exhausting. *Something has to break in order for us to break through.*

I can't help but wonder how often our past hurts stand in the way of our future promised land.

Licensed counselor and author Stephen Arterburn joins me on my radio show periodically. He said this to me one day: "I believe that one of the greatest epidemics in the church today is unresolved grief. We've all walked through a series of heartbreaks and losses that we've never acknowledged or reconciled, and if we have acknowledged them, we've not slowed down long enough to sort through them."

I couldn't help but wonder how all of this unresolved grief has impacted the Body of Christ as a whole, how it's affected our own quality of life, our health, and even our influence. We have an amazing ability to ignore our pain. We stuff it down deep and make Herculean efforts to forget about it. We have a perpetual tendency to treat surface symptoms, never really getting to the root causes of our injuries.

Yet the way of healing is often slow, deep, purposeful, and humbling. And who wants to go there? I'd say the one who's willing to believe that God has restoration, healing, and wholeness waiting for them on the other side. He does, you know.

Spiritual director Beth Allen Slevcove joined me on the show one day to talk about her book *Broken Hallelujahs*. I thought this was fascinating. She explained how our laments actually tell a story. She shared how often people lament over the ways they fall short in life. *I don't pray enough, read enough, exercise enough, etc.* Beth at first listens to the lament that surfaces, but then she probes deeper and asks a few questions. *Almost without fail she finds a true loss beneath the surface lament.* Something that person didn't even realize was there. Maybe they remembered a particular incident but didn't fully grasp how it affected them—and *still* affects them today.

In other words, buried underneath your self-contempt may be a loss you endured when someone abandoned you or let you down. Underneath your chronic sense of imperfection could be an embedded memory of a time when someone held you to an impossible standard. Maybe you hate yourself for your tendency to eat too much of all the wrong things. But might there be, buried underneath, a memory of a time that you should have received comfort, but you didn't? Do you wonder how God feels about that loss for you? Do you think He holds you in contempt because you have a hurt that you've not been ready to face until now?

I'm not at all trying to put thoughts in your head, but I do want to awaken your heart. What's stuffed down beneath the surface for you? What are your "surface laments" telling you?

Beth said this to me about her own process: "When I was able to honestly acknowledge my need, I awakened to God's presence in this dark place. It was easier not to face the confusion and fear lurking deep within, *but it was not better*. The disconnect kept me from myself, from God, and from those I loved. . . . Sometimes we need to suspend judgment, hold off assumptions, and simply let our stories unfold, trusting as we are able in the *slow work of God*. I am beginning to recognize grief not as an interruption but as a means of transformation and grace. I am beginning to understand that what is in the way is the way."

Think about that for a moment in light of my friend's infertility story. *What was in the way was the way.* She went to counseling to sort through her fears and the pain from her childhood experience. In doing so, she could face the fears of her current circumstance and move forward in faith. And by doing so, God made a way where there was no way. Amazing, yes?

F. B. Meyer writes, "God often guides us through our circumstances. One moment, our way may seem totally blocked, but then suddenly some seemingly trivial incident occurs, appearing as nothing to others but speaking volumes to the keen eye of faith. And sometimes these events are repeated in various ways in response to our prayers. They certainly are not haphazard results of chance but are God opening up the way we should walk, by directing our circumstances. *And they begin to multiply as we advance toward our goal*, just as the lights of a city seem to increase as we speed toward it while traveling at night."[2]

God blesses those who mourn, for they will be comforted.

Matthew 5:4

Need Healing?

My friend was willing to sort through her losses and her heartbreak. And God gently and graciously met her in her grief and vulnerability. He brought healing to the very core of her soul. Then He tended to the deep desires of her heart.

We so often think that if we could just possess what our souls long for, then we'd finally be okay. But for most of us, our hearts need healing and our belief system needs an upgrade before we'll be ready to steward the things we so long for. God knows that we're not actually able to carry certain blessings until our hearts are healed. That's why He first invites us into the healing process.

God knows that we're actually not able to carry certain *blessings* until our hearts are healed. That's why He first invites us into the *healing* process.

My friend is such a trophy of God's grace. When I asked her if I could share her story with you, she humbly smiled and said, "Of course."

If you're in a place of brokenness or barrenness, I pray her story encourages you. She shared some of the best advice she ever received, and I think it may be helpful for you too:

> We can't always predict when the waves of grief will come. But when they do, let them wash over you—let yourself feel them to the core of who you are. Sometimes they might just lap at your ankles, and sometimes they might feel like they are crushing you and breaking you. But when they recede—and they always do—they clear off the shores of your heart. They take out the driftwood and trash and gunk that litters the sand, and they leave room for new life to take root.

In her wonderful book *Beauty Marks*, Linda Barrick walks through a list of indicators that reveal if we may need some extra soul-care and time to heal.

> Like physical wounds, emotional wounds have symptoms. If you've been ignoring the signs or growing numb to your own pain, I'd like to share some tools to diagnose a soul wound. This is an opportunity for you to courageously identify what hurts. Pain isn't your enemy. It's your ally in finding the real problem. Trusting God to guide you, look for clues that may signal unresolved wounds. I know this can be rough, *but good is coming*. Here are ten symptoms that can help you identify wounds that need healing in your life:

1. You avoid specific places
2. You avoid certain people
3. You have made a silent inner vow
4. You suffer from emotional triggers
5. You engage in addictive behaviors or have an unhealthy attachment
6. You wound others
7. You experience ongoing, unresolved grief
8. Your thoughts bully you
9. You have a secret you've never told anyone
10. You struggle to verbalize your hurt.

Now picture Jesus Himself holding your face in both of His nail-scarred hands and looking directly into your eyes. Hear Him say to you, "*I love you. I see you. I hear your cries. I remember you. I will take on your pain. I will heal you.*" Let those words soak into your soul![3]

If you're in a season of unearthing, I encourage you to see a godly counselor or mentor to help you walk through some of the things that are surfacing for you. But do know this: Even though the very thought of facing some of these wounds feels like an impossible task, it's not impossible. Nothing is impossible. Your heavenly Father is right beside you. The Spirit of the living God dwells within you. And the Son of God won a *sound* victory for you. All of heaven is on your side.

Jesus never intends to leave us in the valley. We walk *through* the valley of the shadow and we get to the other side. *There is much good waiting for you.* Keep marching. Keep believing. Keep trusting.

Ways We Deal

Getting well takes time and attention. There's a measure of maturity we cannot know until we tend to the issues of our soul. Why are so few willing to do the hard inner work for the sake of freedom? Probably because it's hard. And it's invisible stuff—easy to ignore with so many visible, tangible issues screaming for our attention. But like Beth Allen Slevcove said, it may be easier, but it's not better. I'm so grateful we're taking this journey together.

I'm Grieving

Behold, You desire truth in the inward parts,
And in the hidden part You will make me to know wisdom.

Psalm 51:6 NKJV

What are some of the ways we bypass and/or sabotage our own healing process?

- We stuff and numb (captive).
- We deny and deflect (trigger sensitive).
- We rehearse and rehash (victim mindset).

We stuff and numb (captive): When we refuse to face the hurts in our heart and we shove them down into our soul to deal with later, and then we push them down further with our favorite distraction, we give those *living wounds* no choice but to enter into our physiology so they can get our attention another way. To make matters worse, when we repeatedly turn to our counterfeit comfort to numb our pain, we not only postpone our healing, but we also ensure our own captivity. Scripture tells us that the heavens gasp at the sight of us drinking from broken cisterns (or muddy wells) when the true, living, pure, healing answer is right in front of us. Postponing our grief keeps us from having to feel and deal with pain now, but it's like trading our birthright for a bowl of soup. We give up so much when we refuse to face the ache in our soul and the hunger in our hearts.

"Has anyone ever heard of anything as strange as this?

Has any nation ever traded its gods for new ones, even though they are not gods at all?

Yet my people have exchanged their glorious God for worthless idols! The heavens are shocked at such a thing and shrink back in horror and dismay," says the Lord.

"For my people have done two evil things: They have abandoned me—the fountain of living water. And they have dug for themselves cracked cisterns that can hold no water at all!"

Jeremiah 2:10–13

We deny and deflect (trigger sensitive): When we "stuff and numb" our pain, we get pretty good at denying and deflecting our issues if any person, word, or circumstance gets too close to those hurts. We become proficient at changing the subject, maybe to an area of strength or performance where we seem to be excelling at the moment; or maybe to the flaws of another because they seem to be tripping up at the moment. Another way we deny and deflect is when we point out and tend to the needs of others. (This one makes us seem very spiritual.) Scripture does say that we're to prefer others ahead of ourselves, but Jesus intended for us to do so with a full, free, and whole heart. Yet too often we hide in our service, we numb out on Christian activity while our souls are starving for attention. You know you're serving someone out of a full heart when it really doesn't matter if they notice or acknowledge your humble gift because the focus is on them, and on Jesus, not on yourself. But if, when you prefer others, your goal is to protect *you*, you might want to look at that. And if by preferring others you've managed yet again to keep your hurts hidden and certain people at bay, well then you know that—like the woman at the well in John chapter 4—you need an encounter with Jesus.

Also, when we repeatedly deny and deflect our pain, we become increasingly trigger sensitive (the seemingly smallest things set us off). We put so much energy into self-preservation that the devil can't help but to leverage our sensitivity to his advantage. He orchestrates scenarios to keep us on edge. He purposefully stirs us up. Then he accuses us for our selfish ways. And we agree with him because we wonder why we can't get free. All the while, Jesus waits in the wings and asks, "Do you want to be well?" One last important note on this point: When we deny and deflect our pain, we're not the only ones who lose. We have a sphere of influence. God intends for our life, our journey to impact many people. By taking matters into our own hands and white-knuckling our hurts, we keep others from knowing the God who heals us.

Many of the Samaritans from that village committed themselves to him because of the woman's witness: "He knew all about the things I did. He knows me inside and out!" They asked him to stay on, so Jesus stayed two days. A lot more people entrusted their lives to him when they heard what he had to say. They said to the woman, "We're no longer taking this on your say-so. We've heard it for ourselves and know it for sure. He's the Savior of the world!"

John 4:39–42 THE MESSAGE

We rehearse and rehash (victim mindset): While the first two mindsets can intermingle with each other, this particular mindset tends to stand alone. We become victim-minded when we rehearse and rehash our hurts as a way of life. We think we're dealing with them—because they stay at the forefront of our minds—when in fact we're still reeling from them. If, years after the event, we're more stuck than we've ever been, we can know that our current modus operandi isn't serving us well. But God designed us to thrive.

There's a process in our brains called *neuroplasticity*. It refers to the brain's ability to change—in effect, teaching an old brain new tricks. Our brains (and our bodies) are wired to respond to our most consistent thoughts (and choices). When we keep certain negative, self-focused, self-destructive thoughts on repeat, our brain hardwires that circuit, which makes it easier, faster, and more efficient to hop on that train and go for a ride. But where is it taking us? Remember the phrase I mentioned in an earlier chapter? *Nerves that fire together, wire together.* We need a new train of thought. We need to be transformed by changing the way we think (see Romans 12:2). No one can do this for us.

The Bible tells us that goodness and mercy follow us (Psalm 23), which, to me, indicates that God not only has my back, He redeems my past. When I look over my shoulder at the road I've been on, when I consider what I've done and what's been done to me, and I bring Jesus right into the middle of that mess, I see Him do a work beyond anything I could dare to ask or imagine. And I learn afresh that my Redeemer has mastered the art of redemption. He can take broken pieces, selfish motives, and endless self-preservation and forgive, heal, redeem, and restore. Oh, what a Savior! As Christians, we have no business looking at anyone, anything, or any memory unless we do so through the lens of faith. You may or may not know if you're a "rehearse and rehasher," so I dare you to ask someone close to you. It might be painful to hear, but it's a first step toward healing. Or maybe you already know where your rogue thoughts go, and you know things need to change. Either way, look up and determine to take a more life-giving path than the one you're on.

As you practice a zero-tolerance policy when it comes to victim-thinking, and as you replace that brain space with thoughts of gratitude, joy, and hope, new neural-circuits start to form, creating a new pathway for you to travel on—one that leads you to a place of healing. Christian psychiatrist and brain specialist Dr. Timothy Jennings writes, "As we exercise healthy neural circuits, *these circuits develop, strengthen, and expand.* Conversely, the brain prunes unhealthy circuits when we leave them idle."[4] Did you catch that?

As you practice biblical thinking, your body enforces your healthy choice and helps you by turning your lone path through the woods into a four-lane highway. When you practice healthy thinking, over time, your healthy thoughts become almost instinctive. Amazing, yes? And look at the last line in Dr. Jennings's quote: "Conversely, the brain prunes unhealthy circuits when we leave them idle."

Do you remember that scene in *The Wizard of Oz* when the house fell on the witch and her feet shriveled, rolled up under the house, and disappeared? That's what I picture happening in my brain when I neglect the unhealthy circuits I've traveled on for so long. I pray you're as motivated as I am to work with your body and brain to move toward a healthy, free, healed mindset.

Christa Black Gifford writes:

Your body is linked to your brain, and your brain is linked to your heart. As your heart becomes the primary focus of your life and you learn how to keep it connected and turned into intimacy, your mind naturally changes. Your brain actually rewires, and your physical composition manifests the healing power of *sozo*—the fullness of salvation.[5]

Friends, when life gets really difficult, don't jump to the conclusion that God isn't on the job. Instead, be glad that you are in the very thick of what

Christ experienced. This is a spiritual refining process, with glory just around the corner.

1 Peter 4:12–13 The Message

When you consider that eternity is immeasurable—longer than millions of years—and our life on earth is like a pinprick of time comparably, how do you want to process your wounds? I want to be whole so I can love well. I want to be brave so I can attempt things I never dreamed possible. I want to be free so I can secure freedom for others.

Pursue Healing ~ Pray for a Miracle
Put It into Practice

Focus on . . .

Moving Through Grief

Scripture Says . . .

You have turned my mourning into joyful dancing.
You have taken away my clothes of mourning
and clothed me with joy,
that I might sing praises to you and not be silent.
O Lord my God, I will give you thanks forever!

Psalm 30:11–12

Science Says . . .

Allowing sorrow to spiral into clinical depression is not a healthy option. The stress hormones that can be beneficial in the short term can turn on us in the long term, eventually affecting the hardwiring of the brain. "In the process," says [Stefan] Klein, "the brain loses its adaptability." Even worse, "if this condition is prolonged, the consequences can be devastating: gray cells shrink. . . . Other parts of the brain lose so much matter that they just shrivel up."[6]

Activity—any activity—helps against sadness. You take up life's reins again. When you do something, you engage your brain and deprive it of the opportunity to go down thought's darker paths.[7]

Pursue Healing

We need to feel it to heal it. Maybe you've postponed your grief by stuffing your hurts and heartbreaks. If that's you, I encourage you to pursue a mentor or a counselor and dare to revisit some of the hurts that fester beneath the surface. You will move through it and come out to a place of joy and thanksgiving.

If you've gone around this mountain one too many times and still can't seem to get a breakthrough, I'd suggest trying something new. Read books on the love of God. Memorize whole passages on God's love and compassion and pray them constantly. Keep a thankfulness journal. Ask God to show you if there's a core belief in you that has become an obstacle for you.

Healing is on the horizon for you.

Ask God to show you what next place in you He wants to heal.

Pray for a Miracle

Father, I come to You with all of who I am. You know where I've been, what I've done, and what's been done to me. Heal me, Lord! Reach into those deep places within me and put Your healing balm on my wounds. Show me where I've allowed myself to get stuck and help me break free. Tell me the truth about my sadness and give me perspective on my hurts. My story is not over yet. Help me break through my own scar tissue so I can enjoy new spacious places with You. In Your miracle-working, mighty name I pray. Amen.

Soul Searching

What do your surface laments tell you? What experience, loss, or disappointments have you yet to grieve?

_____

_____

_____

_____

_____

_____

> Lord, I thank you that You are a Promise Maker and a
> Promise Keeper. When I go out to my barren field with a
> sob in my throat and tears in my eyes, and I plant seeds
> of faith in the ground, I can know that after a time, one
> day, I will walk that field and it will be fertile and bursting
> with life. I will remember the days that I wept and walked,
> sowed and waited, and I will rejoice because You have
> kept Your promise to me! I will rejoice as I return to share
> with others the harvest I carry in my arms.
>
> Psalm 125:5–6 (paraphrase)

Prayer

_Father in heaven, I worship You! You have ransomed my life from
the pit. You have saved my soul. And You are redeeming my story.
Help me to trust You with every hidden hurt, every embedded fear,
and every unhealthy way that I process these things. You have a_

better way of life for me. You have new places of promise for me. You will turn my mourning into dancing, my sorrow into true, pure joy. Help me to trust You in the meantime. Have Your way in me, Lord. Show me the hurts that I've worked so hard to hide. Show me a healthy way to process them. Give me a vision for what awaits me on the other side. Help me to discern the enemy's lies so I can shut him down and trust You even more. I am determined to be free. And no one is more committed to my freedom than You are. With my hand in Yours, I will move forward in this process. Show me what's true, and right, and good, and help me to saturate my mind with these things. I'm ready to be made new. Thank you, Jesus. Amen.

Life Reflection

1. Earlier in the chapter I asked you what your surface laments are telling you. Spend more time here exploring that thought. When it comes to lament or complaint, to hurts and loss, where do your thoughts most typically go?

2. Prayerfully ask God to help you identify the deeper loss here. When did that sense of loss first enter your story? Write down your thoughts.

3. Look again at the personalized passage above (Psalm 126:5–6) and write out your own version of this passage. Ask God for the faith to believe that it's true *for you*.

4. What tends to be your way of dealing with your hurts (stuff and numb, deny and deflect, rehearse and rehash)? Be as honest as you're able. How has this process impacted you? Are you ready for something new?

5. Write out a prayer inviting God into those deep places you've not yet visited with Him. Ask Him to give you peace and courage, insight and wisdom. He will.

Spiritual Reset

PRAISE

"Our self-talk is critical to our ability to thrive and flourish, especially when life is hard. When we tell ourselves, 'I'm not going to make it through this,' it's like telling our brains to shut down."[8]

PRAISE—Acronym Exercise

P—Praise Him. Write out a prayer of thanksgiving just because He is God.

_____

_____

_____

R—Remember and Repent. Write out a memory of God's faithfulness. Spend time with Him and repent of anything He brings to mind.

_____

_____

_____

A—Ask Him for what's on your heart.

_____

_____

_____

I—Intercede for others.

_____

_____

_____

S—Stand on God's promises. Write out a promise that under-girds what you're asking Him for.

_____

_____

_____

E—Eternity. Put your life, your burdens, and your prayer list up to the lens of eternity. Ask Jesus to help you look up and think long, with eternity in mind.

_____

_____

_____

Digging Deeper

*Use your journal or notebook for this section.

A. One of my favorite go-to verses on the topic of inner healing is Psalm 147:3–4: "He heals the brokenhearted and bandages their wounds. He counts the stars and calls them all by name." This verse reminds me that the One who put the stars in place knows very well how to heal me in a way that makes me flourish. He's near enough to be intimately aware of our hurts, and He's mighty enough to manage unknown galaxies. That's our God. Write out a personalized version of this amazing passage.

B. Read Psalm 77 (the whole chapter) and note the verse where this prayer changes from lament and loss of perspective to faith and rehearsing God's promise. What did the psalmist do to find his footing again? (Hint: see verses 11–12.) Write down your thoughts.

C. Think about a time when you pulled yourself out of a thought-funk and remembered afresh God's faithfulness to you. How did that change things for you? Write out a prayer of thanksgiving and faith—declaring who God has been to you and who He will be for you in the days ahead.

D. Read Isaiah 53:3–6 and consider the pain and grief Jesus bore, and how He was utterly misjudged for His suffering. He knows how you feel. And even more than that, He took the power away from the enemy. Yes, the devil can hurt us, but he can no longer harm us. Even our pain and our losses will make us richer in Christ when we trust Him. We cannot fathom the highway of holiness that Jesus has paved for us. He made a way where there was no way. Now, freedom, wholeness, and healing are possible.

Write out a prayer thanking Jesus for His indescribable gift; ask Him to show you how to pursue your unique path of healing. Ask Him for a miracle.

> **Find the following downloadable print at SusieLarson.com.**

I WANT TO BE WHOLE

so I can love well.

I WANT TO HAVE VISION

so I will dare to dream.

I WANT TO BE BRAVE

so I will attempt the impossible.

I WANT TO BE FREE

so I can help win freedom for others.

CHAPTER

seven

I'm Discouraged

Jesus, Change My Perspective

Be strong and take heart, all you who hope in the Lord.

Psalm 31:24 NIV

Spring will be a season when new beauty grows in our lives in ways we cannot imagine right now. We can wait for it with glad wonder. We can wait for it with renewed joy. We can wait for the day we will bloom.[1]

REMEMBER A DAY during a difficult season when God broke through the dark clouds of disappointment that hovered overhead. Facedown on the floor, I sobbed ugly tears. I could barely catch my breath. I choked out questions like "How did this happen, Lord? Why did this happen?"

Right there in the middle of my despair the Lord whispered His wisdom to me: *"Susie, you're asking the wrong questions."* And I was. Those questions only deepened my sense of despair. I sat up, wiped my tears, and whispered back, "So what are the *right* questions, Lord?" He gave me three questions to ask myself that forever changed the way I process and frame my disappointments. They are:

- *What is this disappointment saying* to me *that's not true?*
- *What is this disappointment saying* about me *that's not true?*
- *What is this disappointment saying* to me about God *that's not true?*[2]

When we allow our disappointments to cloud our view and our negative conclusions to go unchallenged, our perspective will always be skewed. We can't see clearly when our faith-lens is smeared with lies.

If you're battling discouragement or disappointment, I encourage you to prayerfully spend some time with these questions. Search your Bible. Ask God for a fresh perspective. See if He doesn't bring truth right into the middle of your circumstance.

The Faces of Discouragement

When life doesn't quite turn out the way we thought or hoped it would, we battle discouragement. We may even lose hope. Sometimes our heartbreak sits so close to the surface that it feels like we're bleeding under our armor. How can that not impact our perspective?

Then there's the long, drawn-out battle. When the storms rage on and we see no end in sight, it can be exhausting and discouraging.

When we feel misjudged or misunderstood, it's downright hurtful and discouraging.

When our loved ones struggle, wander, or wade into the waters of apathy, we experience fear, worry, and despair. Hard to watch when we know God has so much more for them.

Sometimes, though, we're the cause of our own despair. We beat ourselves up over our imperfections. We hold ourselves to a standard that we'd never ask of others. Or we're just stuck and can't seem to move forward because of past sins or missteps.

Another way we cause self-induced discouragement is by wrongly framing our story or by white-knuckling our unrealistic expectations.

I'm Discouraged

Most of us are far more blessed than we realize. Yet when we zero in on a certain point of disappointment, we miss the abundance all around us. We compare and despair. We believe what we see on social media and forget that everybody hurts, everybody has messes, and everybody needs a Savior.

I know, for me, I had an unrealistic picture of what my sons' faith journeys should look like once they became young adults. I soon realized that God's promises don't apply to my own unrealistic expectations. His promises apply to my impossible situations. These are two totally different things.

We read in Romans 4 how Abraham faced the fact that his body was as good as dead, but he did not waver in unbelief regarding the promises of God. That's sturdy faith in the face of the facts. Whereas when we despair over our disappointment and that disappointment comes from an expectation based on fantasy, then we need a reset before we can fully engage our faith.

God's *promises* don't apply to my own unrealistic *expectations*. His promises apply to my impossible situations. These are two totally *different* things.

For example, let's say you're married to a decent guy but your marriage lacks the zeal and passion you long for. You read racy romance novels and relentlessly watch other "perfect couples" from a distance and before you know it, you find yourself constantly critical of your own marriage. Your unhealthy perspective forges an unhealthy thought pattern that plays on repeat. Those repetitive thoughts eventually cause you to despair and look around for other options. Suddenly you come to believe that there's really nothing good or salvageable in your marriage. And instead of asking God for a miracle, you linger around your disappointment until finally you tell yourself that you deserve better than this. You create an alternate reality, which eventually leads to destructive choices that you cannot undo.

I've talked with women who've walked this path. They'd give anything to go back and engage some radical faith for their marriage. They've shared how in hindsight, as it turned out, their lives and marriages weren't nearly as terrible as they perceived them to be.

For faith to work, we need to face the facts—to see things as they are, and not as they seem, or even as we think they should be. And, amidst our hurt, to be able to see how truly rich we are in Christ (and to acknowledge how profoundly He's already blessed us). We also need to see and acknowledge the depth of our neediness before Him. And when it comes to our heartbreak, we need to admit our shortcomings, own our part.

We'll never get anywhere in life by demanding things from God, or by constantly blaming others and refusing to look at ourselves, or by striving in our own strength in an effort to force an outcome. To thrive amidst our disappointments, we need to be humble, teachable, and grateful. We need to believe that God knows what He's doing. We need to embrace the fact that we see only a portion of the whole story. There's so much we don't know, so many things we perceive incorrectly. Thus, we need to be willing—with God's help—to learn new ways to navigate our hurts and frame our perspective. Jesus will show us His way. There is no other way.

This is the essence of entrusting our very real and imperfect lives to a perfect, powerful God.

So how do we navigate through our disappointments with a right perspective and a heart full of faith? I use the letters ABCD to find perspective in the face of hurts and heartbreaks:

- **Acknowledge** that you're an heir
- **Bring** your blessings into view
- **Claim** the power and the potency of God's promises
- **Die** to self wherever you need to

Acknowledge That You're an Heir

I spent the better part of my book *Your Powerful Prayers* exploring what it means to be an heir of God and why our status makes a world of difference in how we approach His throne to address the concerns of our hearts.

Check it out if you need a fresh reminder of what it means to belong to the Most High God. But in the meantime, here's a short excerpt that speaks to the blessing of our heir status:

> The truth of the matter is, as heirs of God and joint heirs with Christ, we have certain privileges. We have His presence, His promises, and His power. *Let that sink in for a moment.* In fact, let me say it again: We have His presence—His holy, awe-inspiring presence where the fullness of joy is found. We have His promises—His faithful, true promises that change everything for the Christ-follower. And we have His power—the same power that rose Christ from the dead, available to us. We're more spiritual than physical, more found than lost, and more loved than we know. Isn't that just something?
>
> And though we face giants who aim to destroy us, and an enemy who's always in a bad mood, we serve a joy-filled, patient, kind, and loving Father who always leads us triumphantly through our battles.[3]

When disappointment clouds your view, stop right where you are and remind yourself *whose* you are. Picture yourself at the royal table of grace not because you've earned it, but because Christ has earned it for you. Remind your soul that you lack no good thing, because you have Jesus. And He happens to be the God who fights for you. You're not alone in your trials, and those very trials will serve you well in the end if you'll be trained by them. Spend some time with Him around this idea of your royal identity.

> And since we are his children, we are his heirs. In fact, together with Christ we are heirs of God's glory. But if we are to share his glory, we must also share his suffering.

Romans 8:17

Bring Your Blessings into View

I know that when I find myself careening for the ditch of disappointment, it's because I've taken my eyes off of Jesus, which makes me also lose sight of the many blessings He's already provided in my life.

Have you ever seen one of those movies when the camera zooms in fast on a person and it makes everything else in the peripheral go blurry? That's what disappointment does to our perspective. And the enemy wants it that way. But he's not the boss of our perspective. We are. Maybe it's time to look around and bring your blessings back into focus. Notice them. Speak them aloud. Imagine how you'd feel if they went away tomorrow. Thank God for the nuances of the things that mean so much to you. Linger around your blessings and look at them from different angles. For example, spend some time thanking Jesus for the systems in your body that automatically work whether you notice or not. Thank Him for the miraculous morning sunrise that reminds you of His fresh and new mercies. Doing this on a regular basis will heal your soul and restore your perspective.

When we step back and take inventory of the boundary lines that make up our lives, we can say with the psalmist

> O Lord, You are the portion of my inheritance and my cup;
> You maintain my lot.
> The lines have fallen to me in pleasant places;
> Yes, I have a good inheritance.
>
> I will bless the Lord who has given me counsel;
> My heart also instructs me in the night seasons.
> I have set the Lord always before me;
> Because He is at my right hand I shall not be moved.
>
> Psalm 16:5–8 NKJV

One day when I knew I needed a reset, I spent some time pondering my place at the table of grace. Then I began to look around within my lot lines and suddenly felt overwhelmed by God's goodness to me. I marveled at how patient He is with us! Sometimes I feel like the child who's so wrapped up in her angst about a knot in her shoelace that she's forgotten that she's standing in line at Disneyland.

Listen, I'm not saying that our troubles are trite. But we certainly make little of our blessings (we make them trite) by focusing too much on our unfulfilled desires, our hurts, and our disappointments. There's a way to live in the tension of today's blessings and burdens and tomorrow's promises and breakthroughs. May Jesus show us how to stay humbly grateful and hopefully expectant.

Here's an excerpt from my journal:

Dear Father, with all my heart, I thank You for how You've guided and provided, for what You've purposed and what You've prevented, for what You've granted and what You've withheld. All of these reveal Your goodness to me. You have so strategically and wisely led me and loved me that it leaves me breathless. How can I ever thank You enough? Help me to live a life worthy of Your name. In Your mighty name I pray. Amen.

Always be joyful. Never stop praying. Be thankful in all circumstances, for this is God's will for you who belong to Christ Jesus.

1 Thessalonians 5:16–18

Claim the Power and Potency of God's Promises

We lose perspective when we loosen our hold on God's promises. We lose perspective when we zero in on our hurts to the point that we no longer remember all we possess simply because we have Jesus. How do we find clarity again? First, we remind ourselves who we are because of whose we are. We are heirs of God, joint heirs with Christ. Then, we tell our souls that the blood will never lose its power! God's promises are as potent as they've ever been. The gospel is not old news, it's now news; it's the best news! We remind ourselves that all of heaven is on our side and all of God's promises are yes, and amen.[4]

If you've lost vision for your life, if you've lost hope and perspective, it might be time to apply the passage below to your current circumstances. Our story is bigger than we are. People are watching us, waiting to see how we'll sort through our hardships and disappointments. They're waiting to see if our faith is real.

So take a new grip with your tired hands and strengthen your weak knees. Mark out a straight path for your feet so that those who are weak and lame will not fall but become strong.

Hebrews 12:12–13

Maybe it's time to grab hold of God's promises that are specific to your situation.[5] Maybe it's time to grab your trembling knees and tell your legs to *be strong* in the strength of the Lord. Keep walking. God will give you strength as you go.

Maybe it's time to get a fresh vision for where God is taking you. Find out what obedience looks like for you in this particular season and set your face like flint on the path God has for you. As you apply yourself to God's purposes in this difficult season, others will notice and be strengthened too. Your faith affects your own story and the greater story God is writing on the earth today. Be strong in the Lord and put your trust in Him.

Die to Self Wherever You Need To

In order for us to find hope again—the kind of hope that heals and purifies us from the inside out—we must submit ourselves to the searching work of the Holy Spirit. When our disappointments surface, so do the things in our character that need to go—things like entitlement, selfishness, and ingratitude. All of these are displayed in our tendency to compare and then despair, or to gripe and complain.

If we're not careful, our heartbreak will make us selfish, self-focused people. Our grief turns to self-pity, our world shrinks, and everybody notices but us. We'll never fully find perspective amidst our hurts or sort through our disappointments unless we're willing to acknowledge, take responsibility for, and then surrender the parts of us that Jesus wants to redeem.

This isn't about condemnation. It's about invitation: the invitation to die to our inner lawyer's desire to self-defend and self-justify; to our imagined rights and selfish demands that compel us to believe we should be more privileged than another; and to the self-pity that keeps us stuck in the pit.

I'm Discouraged

When we *die* to the very things that threaten to destroy us, God's Spirit lives more *valiantly* through us. And when that happens, we are *awakened* and others are blessed.

We have to die to the destructive parts of ourselves so we can live more fully in the power of the Holy Spirit.

Life in Christ makes us full and free, rich and true. It's the narcissist turned heir who now serves at the homeless shelter. It's the former anorexic who can now sit down and enjoy a delicious piece of pie with her family. It's the former workaholic who comes in the door after work and happily knows how to drop his sword so he can pick up his kids. It's the once insecure woman who now takes audacious risks on the other side of the world, all for the kingdom.

When we die to the very things that threaten to destroy us, God's Spirit lives more valiantly through us. And when that happens, we are awakened and others are blessed.

> People imagine that dying to self makes one miserable. But it is just the opposite. It is the refusal to die to self that makes one miserable. The more we know of death with Him, the more we shall know of His life in us, and so the more of real peace and joy.[6]

He's Always Up to Something *New*

Right in the face of your disappointments, our star-breathing God invites you to sing a *new* song, to pray a *fresh* prayer, to secure a *redeemed* perspective. When you engage with Him in this way—when you love Him with all your heart, mind, soul, and strength—you honor Him. And in the process, He somehow naturally and supernaturally changes *you*.

God is always up to something new. And wherever you've been in life, whatever thoughts you've had on repeat, know this: *He has wired you for newness.*

- Outwardly, we naturally age, but inwardly we're supernaturally *renewed* day by day—2 Corinthians 4:16

- He's made us *new* creations—2 Corinthians 5:17
- He's given us a *new* heart and a *new* spirit—Ezekiel 36:26
- His mercies are *new* every morning—Lamentations 3:20–22
- He offers *new* strength—Isaiah 40:31
- He's given us a *new* attitude and a new self—Ephesians 4:22–24
- He's doing a *new* thing and making a *new* way (one that wasn't there before)—Isaiah 43:19

Lance Hahn, author of *The Master's Mind*, joined me on the show a while back. He offers an important perspective here:

> Much of what we define as suffering comes from a distorted perspective.
> . . . I wonder how many of us fully understand the power of our thoughts.
> Do we realize that what we think, we will ultimately do? There is no action
> that is not preceded by a thought. The human body is designed with a com-
> mand center called the brain, and every system takes its control from that
> center. If we want to bring change to our lives—and who doesn't?—we must
> master things here first.[7]

Though Scripture tells us that we're changed by the renewing of our minds (Romans 12:2), and I've practiced redeemed thinking for years, it wasn't until I learned how profoundly our bodies respond to our most consistent thoughts that I felt the deep conviction to put even more effort into the perspective that I attach to my circumstances. In other words, I'm quicker to challenge my instinctive perspective, especially if it pulls my gaze downward.

If we allow our disappointments and discouragements to stay at the forefront of our minds—unchallenged and unfiltered—our perspective will become increasingly negative, and our lives progressively unhealthy.

Disappointment and discouragement are tough on our systems. They cause our muscles to tense and our cells to self-protect, making it difficult to receive proper nourishment from food. We don't hydrate as well when we're bogged down with despair. We don't sleep as well either, which profoundly affects the healing and repair process in our bodies. Discouragement also has a way of

I'm Discouraged

pulling our gaze to the ground. Forget about vision; we don't even have perspective. And the enemy wants it that way. But remember what Scripture says?

> Where there is no vision from God, the people run wild,
> but those who adhere to God's instruction know genuine happiness.
>
> Proverbs 29:18 THE VOICE

Here's the *Amplified* version of this same passage:

> Where there is no vision [no revelation of God and His word], the people are unrestrained;
> But happy and blessed is he who keeps the law [of God].

Another translation of this passage says that *without vision, people cast off all restraint.* When we see no way out, we stop pressing in. When we despair, we tend to allow ourselves indulgences that temporarily numb our discomfort because survival becomes our main goal. When we surrender to our circumstances rather than surrendering to God in our circumstances, we passively go with the flow and call it meekness.

But when we consistently remember God's faithfulness and rehearse His promises, when we apply His truth to our lives, and when we consistently make healthy life-adjustments, the narrative changes in our brains and our physiology, and those messages work their way out into our emotions, our perspective, and our reality.

But faith holds unswervingly to the promise (Hebrews 10:23), believes in spite of the odds (Hebrews 11:1), and dreams new dreams (Hebrews 11:6) in the face of frustration, fear, disappointment, and discouragement. You've heard this oft-quoted passage from the prophet Jeremiah:

> "For I know the plans I have for you," declares the Lord, "plans to prosper you and not to harm you, plans to give you hope and a future."
>
> Jeremiah 29:11 NIV

This is such an encouraging passage—one that fits well on memes and greeting cards—but we often forget that God sent this message to a people in *exile*. In fact, earlier in the chapter, God told them to plan for the future in the face of their current hardship. Let's take a look at the charge God gave His people:

> Build houses and settle down; plant gardens and eat what they produce. Marry and have sons and daughters; find wives for your sons and give your daughters in marriage, so that they too may have sons and daughters. Increase in number there; do not decrease. Also, seek the peace and prosperity of the city to which I have carried you into exile. Pray to the Lord for it, because if it prospers, you too will prosper.
>
> Jeremiah 29:5–7 NIV

Picture, if you can, Jesus walking right into the middle of your circumstance and passionately imploring you, *I want you to dream here. I want you to feast here. I want you to increase, not decrease here. I want you to be a blessing to those around you. I am doing a new thing. It won't always be this way. You don't see it clearly now, but will you trust me? Soon, and very soon, you will see the new thing I'm about to do for you. Guard your heart here, hold fast to the promise here, guard your mind here, learn to flourish here, and remember what's true here, even when it doesn't feel true.*

We don't flourish in our hardships by wallowing in them. Nor do we flourish in our hardships by ignoring them. We flourish when we face what breaks our heart, and then we look up to Jesus, the keeper of our hearts. As we cooperate with Him, He helps us sort through our story in the most healing way possible. We flourish when we abide in Christ. We flourish when we steward what He has entrusted to us. And we flourish when we ruthlessly banish the attitudes and thoughts that only weaken us. We've got to develop a backbone when it comes to the enemy and his plans to destroy us.

One of the muscles God strengthened in me through my health battle was my "NO!" muscle. Ephesians 6 tells us about the weapons of our warfare. Ephesians 6:16 talks about the shield of faith God has given us to extinguish *every* fiery dart the enemy sends our way. In my season of suffering, it seemed that the enemy had constant and open access to me (he didn't, but it felt that way). Arrows zinged by me from every angle.

It wasn't until I started to raise my shield—over and over again, with every arrow, every lie, and every threat—that I got better and better at saying NO! to the enemy of my soul. Like Daniel in the film *Karate Kid*, God had me practice the same moves over and over again (wax on, wax off) until my defensive moves became almost instinctive. Now I sense a lie when it comes my way, and in feisty faith, I say, "No way! I'm not wearing that, carrying it, or even considering it." And I block it with my shield. I can't afford discouragement or despair, especially since God has called us to courage. And while I can't prove this, I get the feeling that our faith-shield grows the more we use it.

With the Spirit of the Living God actively at work within us, we have access to more power and strength and courage than we could ever appropriate. So let's walk in the power of the Holy Spirit so we will not give in to the whims of our self-focused nature. We need God's power, especially when our hearts are breaking.

We're invited to thrive in the not yet. We're invited to grow strong in battle. We're invited to know a peace that surpasses understanding—the kind of other-worldly peace that makes no sense when you consider our circumstances. These are just a few of the countless treasures that belong to us because we belong to Jesus. We can thrive here. So let's thrive here.

Pursue Healing ~ Pray for a Miracle

Put It into Practice

Focus on . . .

Embracing Courage

Scripture Says . . .

"This is my command—be strong and courageous! Do not be afraid or discouraged. For the Lord your God is with you wherever you go."

Joshua 1:9

This seems easier said than done until we ponder the power of Emmanuel: God *With* Us. Whatever comes at you, in whatever ways the enemy tries to threaten you, in whatever storms surround you, God—the keeper of all things—is *with you*. His intent is on *you*. He watches over *you*. Nothing heals the heart like the growing awareness of God's great love for us and His intimate presence with us.

Science Says . . .

Neuroscientists recently determined just how courage works in the brain, finding that a region called the subgenual anterior cingulate cortex (sgACC) is the driving force behind courageous acts— a conclusion which could one day prove useful in treating anxiety disorders.

So how can we train our minds to act more courageously in everyday life? Other recent research on courage, which has shown that it's not just about facing fear, but also about coping with risk and uncertainty

I'm Discouraged

(as Ernest Hemingway put it, courage is "grace under pressure"). And, it seems, we can make ourselves more courageous with practice and effort.[8]

Our thoughts tend to derail in the face of uncertainty. But what if we identified these moments as opportunities to set our faces like flint and *practice courage*? You are a warrior. You're stronger than you know because the great God of heaven resides in your soul. Be courageous!

Pursue Healing

Ask God to show you where you've worked overtime to stay comfortable. Ask Him to show you how to step out of the comfortable so you can practice courage.

Consider your current battle with discouragement as an added opportunity to find the warrior within. Grab hold of faith and determine not to coddle feelings that weaken you.

Think about yourself a year from now: What would a more courageous, audacious you look like?

Jesus has offered you His strength. Now it's yours to lay hold of that strength.

Pray for a Miracle

Father, do a miracle in me! Work in and through me so wildly and wonderfully that when others see me, they decide to run after You! Awaken my heart to all You have for me. Create in me a tenacious, audacious heart to go after all of the freedom You won for me. Help me to face my life with courage in my soul and a fire in my bones. I want to be the brave, bold, beautiful woman You envisioned before time began. Lead me there, Lord. I will follow. In Your matchless name I pray. Amen.

Soul Searching

How often do you think about your disappointments? What thought process would God have you embrace instead?

_____

_____

_____

_____

_____

> Lord, I know that You are kind and have called me to share eternal glory with You. What a wonderful thought! I know You see me. And I know that there's an end date to my suffering. A day is coming when You will stretch out Your hand and put a stop to this trial. At that time, You Yourself will lift me up again; You'll strengthen and support me, deliver and defend me. You will place me on a firm foundation. My soul waits for You!
>
> 1 Peter 5:10 (paraphrase)

Prayer

Precious Lord, I trust You. Forgive me for the countless times I've sulked in my disappointments when I could have stood in faith. Forgive me for the times I've wrapped myself up in self-pity instead of wrapping myself up in Your redeeming grace. You always have much more for me than I can fathom. Help me to walk in Your ways. Open my eyes so I can see things as they are and not as they seem. I want *to view life through Your lens of clarity and compassion, conviction and confidence. You're never afraid, You're never worried, and You never wonder if things will work out. Help me to stand on that higher ground so that my faith perspective brings life to many who need what You so lovingly make available to us. Fill me afresh with Your wonder-working power. My soul waits for You. In Jesus' name I pray. Amen.*

Life Reflection

1. When you consider the varying disappointments you've endured over the years, which one most often surfaces for you?

2. Spend some time with God; walk through the ABCD exercise mentioned earlier in the chapter. Ask God to show you if there's any part of your disappointment that comes from an unrealistic expectation (that's not always the case, but it's worth exploring). Write out your thoughts on this disappointment (why you're disappointed, what God has been saying to you about it, and what you need to do to find perspective before the desire of your heart comes to fruition).

3. In what ways has the enemy tried to leverage your disappointments against you (baited you into repetitive thoughts; tempted you to compare and despair; tempted you to lose vision and disengage from faith, etc.)?

4. We must have the courage to challenge our negative conclusions and be ruthless with our destructive thought patterns. If it applies here, identify any negative conclusions and/or destructive thought patterns that you need to extract from your perspective. Remember, we must not put a period at the end of a sentence that God is still writing.

5. Joy is such an act of faith. Do you think it's possible to entrust your disappointment to the Lord and enjoy your life and your relationship with God in the meantime? What would that look like for you? Write down your thoughts.

Spiritual Reset

PRAISE

As believers, every one of us should live with a central goal for our heart to think, speak, feel, and act in the fluent language of God, which is the language of love. But until every part of our heart is flying the unified flag of love above all pain, trauma, bitterness, and offense, it will continue to spew all sorts of things we would rather it didn't.[9]

PRAISE—Acronym Exercise

P—Praise Him. Write out a prayer of thanksgiving just because He is God.

_____

_____

_____

R—Remember and Repent. Write out a memory of God's faithfulness. Spend time with Him and repent of anything He brings to mind.

_____

_____

_____

A—Ask Him for what's on your heart.

_____

_____

_____

I—Intercede for others.

_____

_____

_____

S—Stand on God's promises. Write out a promise that under-girds what you're asking Him for.

_____

_____

_____

E—Eternity. Put your life, your burdens, and your prayer list up to the lens of eternity. Ask Jesus to help you look up and think long, with eternity in mind.

_____

_____

_____

Digging Deeper

*Use a journal or notebook for this section.

A. Read Psalm 106:24–25 and answer the following questions: (1) Have I disengaged my faith and surrendered to my circumstances? (2) Am I white-knuckling something God wants me to entrust to Him? (3) Is it possible that my disappointments are lying to me? Write down your thoughts.

B. Read Hebrews 12:12–13 and break down this verse into steps of obedience (for your good and for God's glory): (1) What would a "new grip" look like for you? A particular promise, attitude, step of engagement? (2) What would it look like to "strengthen your knees"? (3) What's the path God has set before you? What does obedience look like here, regardless of your flesh, your fears, or your frustrations? What's the straight path that God wants you to identify? (4) Who in your life is most likely watching how you navigate this area of your life? What do you want them to see?

C. Read Hebrews 10:35–36 and consider this: Your holy confidence before God matters deeply to Him, so much so that He takes note and intends to reward you for your faith. Why? Because you become more like Him as you trust Him, and others see Him when they see you. We cannot mature without learning to persevere. It's a critical part of this journey. Write out a faith declaration, telling your soul and your God that you will not relent, fall out, or back down. You're in this for the long haul, and you know that God will strengthen you as you go!

> Find the following downloadable print
> at SusieLarson.com.

FAITH PLANS FOR THE FUTURE
in the face of fear.

FAITH SEES A HARVEST
where barrenness lies.

FAITH ENVISIONS FREEDOM
in the midst of captivity.

FAITH IS
good for my soul.

FAITH BRINGS
joy to my Father's heart.

I WILL ENGAGE MY **FAITH** TODAY.

I'm Insecure

Jesus, Show Me How You See Me

I pray that from his glorious, unlimited resources he will empower you with inner strength through his Spirit. Then Christ will make his home in your hearts as you trust in him. Your roots will grow down into God's love and keep you strong. And may you have the power to understand, as all God's people should, how wide, how long, how high, and how deep his love is. May you experience the love of Christ, though it is too great to understand fully. Then you will be made complete with all the fullness of life and power that comes from God.

Ephesians 3:16–19

If your life is off-key, maybe it's because you've been deafened by the negative self-talk that doesn't let God get a Word in edgewise! Maybe you've listened to the voice of criticism so long you can't believe anything else about yourself. Or maybe it's the Enemy's voice of condemnation that speaks lies about who you really are. If you don't silence those competing voices, they'll eventually deafen you. You won't be able to sing God's song because you won't be able to hear His voice.[1]

*D*R. TROY SAT IN FRONT OF HIS COMPUTER, punched the keys, and opened my file. He looked over the notes from our last appointment, then looked at me and said, "So. How are you feeling today?"

I forced a smile and nodded, and said, "Um. Okay."

His brows furrowed a bit. He swiveled his chair away from his desk and faced me head on. "What's going on, Susie?"

Honestly, I felt silly even bringing up a little head cold, but truth be told, anger, frustration, and sadness all tangled up together inside me and formed a lump in my throat. My surging emotions didn't at all match my circumstances, which embarrassed and confused me.

I answered his question while trying to minimize my ridiculous emotions. "I'm okay, really. Just a little bummed. I've worked so hard to take care of myself. I take my vitamins, go to bed early, drink lots of water, exercise, and build margin into my schedule. I'm doing everything I know to do to stay healthy. I'm about to head into my spring speaking season and I have a scratchy throat. Usually when I feel like this and I have to hit the road, the seemingly harmless scratchy throat turns into a full-blown brutal case of bronchitis or even pneumonia. I feel like I can't win, no matter how hard I try."

Dr. Troy stood up and pointed to the patient table. "Have a seat. We'll get to your symptoms in a moment but I want to talk more about what's brewing under the surface for you."

He paused for a moment, took a deep breath, and took a few steps toward me, then continued, "Susie, just indulge me for a second. Open up your hands and tell God, 'I accept me and I trust You.' Go ahead and say it: '*I accept me and I trust You.*'"

I couldn't speak. My eyes squeezed back tears. I clenched my teeth and shook my head. Then I opened my hands, opened my mouth, and right there in his office, I let out a guttural sob like I've never known before. I held my stomach, doubled over, and released a river of pent-up tears. What in the world was going on with me?

Dr. Troy cocked his head to one side. "Susie, you're a responsible person, I can tell by watching you. And you feel like you let down your sons when you were a young mom battling Lyme disease. And now, all these years later, you're still afraid to let people down. You're mad at yourself because you don't want to disappoint or fail those event hosts. Well, let me tell you, Susie, self-contempt will do more harm to your soul and to your cells than any disease ever could. We're working on your health issues and I believe you'll win this battle, but at some point you have to accept your limits and not berate yourself for the ways you need God in this season. He can work through your weakness. He will show Himself strong on your behalf."

We never enjoy those seasons in life when our emotions seem to have a mind of their own. But like we've discussed throughout this book, *The storms reveal the lies we believe and the truths we need.* That moment in Dr. Troy's office ushered in another D-day victory for me. I experienced a new level of freedom just by identifying the self-contempt that I'd been unaware of until that day.

If you've enjoyed good health most of your life, you might not understand the weariness, the despair, and the emotions one feels when we go for long stretches of time without feeling well. Even so, I'm convinced that God uses everything the enemy sends our way to get at the root of what truly stands in our way of wholeness and healing. Though I had a legitimate reason to be sick and tired of feeling sick and tired, God knew that the underlying issue of self-contempt was deeply hurting me and needed to be extracted from my soul.

That day in my doctor's office, I suddenly felt peace and grace and freedom to simply *be* in the place God had me, and to accept myself with all of my limitations. I'm wondering, might you also need to exercise a little self-compassion for the ways you need God in this particular season of life? Think of it this way: Self-contempt is poison. Self-compassion is medicine. And this is true for all of us: *Every* step toward healing matters.

> At some point you have to accept your *limits* and not berate yourself for the ways you need God in this *season*. He can work through your weakness. He will show Himself *strong* on your behalf.

I'd carried profound angst in my soul and intense frustration in my spirit, not because I lacked the grace to walk through my battle (because I've never lacked the grace to do this journey, God has made sure of that), but because I was so frustrated with my limitations and I truly didn't want to let people down. I'm hyper-responsible to my core.

But I realized at that moment that it went even deeper for me. I couldn't control how others might respond to my weaknesses, and that scared me, frustrated me, and dimmed my view of God's love for me in this place.

Maybe you don't relate to my health struggle but have your own areas in life that frustrate you. Are you unkind to your soul when you eat too much, share too much, spend too much, or leave too much undone at home or at work? Maybe you're continually frustrated with yourself because you just can't seem to get over a broken heart. Perhaps you shake your head in utter disgust when you stare in the mirror at your bumpy thighs or your saggy belly. Or maybe you secretly berate yourself when you don't serve enough, pray enough, give enough, love enough.

We all have raw places in us that need love and healing, not a judge and jury.

Until we learn how to accept ourselves and entrust every part of our souls to Jesus, we will instinctively do everything we can to overcompensate for our shortcomings, cover up our messes, and denigrate ourselves for our weaknesses. Or else we will play the blame game, point the finger, make up excuses, or totally shut down. But can you see how striving, cover-ups, and self-contempt are *not* what we need to heal? Consider the opposites of these three responses:

- Antonyms for Strive: *Rest, Let go, Unwind*
- Antonyms for Cover-Up: *Unveil, Admit, Show*
- Antonym for Self-contempt (I found only one): *Self-love*

Next time you and I are tempted to turn on ourselves, might it be a better idea to go boldly into God's presence? To bow low, unwind, and let go? What if in that place of peace and stillness and soul-safety we dared to trust Him by unveiling those places in us we'd rather not face?

So all of us who have had that veil removed can see and reflect the glory of the Lord. And the Lord—who is the Spirit—makes us more and more like him as we are changed into his glorious image.

2 Corinthians 3:18

What if we showed Him our need and asked Him to show us His love? I don't know about you, but just the thought of it puts my heart at ease. But maybe for you this stirs up more fear than faith. If that's you, I pray Jesus leads you beside still waters and surprises you with a strong sense of His affection, maybe when you least expect it.

Read Eugene Peterson's paraphrase of Romans 8:1–3:

> With the arrival of Jesus, the Messiah, that fateful dilemma is resolved. Those who enter into Christ's being-here-for-us no longer have to live under a continuous, low-lying black cloud. A new power is in operation. The Spirit of life in Christ, like a strong wind, has magnificently cleared the air, freeing you from a fated lifetime of brutal tyranny at the hands of sin and death.
>
> God went for the jugular when he sent his own Son. He didn't deal with the problem as something remote and unimportant. In his Son, Jesus, he personally took on the human condition, entered the disordered mess of struggling humanity in order to set it right once and for all.

THE MESSAGE

Doesn't that passage make you want to stand up and shout? Jesus not only entered into our mess, He took the enemy's "right" to accuse us and blew it to smithereens!

The enemy aims to taunt, threaten, and diminish us because of our humanity, but we are not obligated to listen to him! Jesus not only won the victory for us, He also has offered to meet us—profoundly so—right in the midst of our greatest need. He's made us perfect while He's making us holy (see Hebrews 10:14). As we behold Him, we become like Him (see 2 Corinthians 3:18).

In her beautiful book *Ruthless: Knowing the God Who Fights For You*, Bo Stern writes:

I know I am small. And in the face of an Everest-sized battle, my faith often seems smaller than small. But God does not reject my too-little faith. Instead, He breathes His strength into the seed and allows me to share the thrill of His supernatural resourcefulness. In a world that relentlessly reduces us to skin and bones, our God speaks abundant, outrageous life. He creates. He renovates. He turns trash into treasure, fish into feast, and a nearly invisible grain of faith into a mountain-moving force. He speaks, and beauty grows wild on our battlefield, causing giants to fall and joy to rise. He moves, and hope runs loose through broken dreams, breathing life where death once danced. He is the God of more-than-enough. Believe it.[2]

God doesn't fear our messes. He's moved by them. And to prove it, He was born in the womb of a teenage girl, entered the world in a poor, smelly stable, and lay down for a nap in a feeding trough. The glory of God came to earth because we desperately needed redemption. And now we have it, praise God!

Jesus speaks life. He breathes life. When He looks at us, He sees beauty, potential, and worth. And He invites us to *agree* with Him.

We are all a pile of contradictions. I often say that we are works in progress, and we get to be, *without the condemnation.*

Yet, on the healing journey, our stuff will emerge. God allows our hurts to surface at precisely the right time (when He knows we're ready). With every new layer of need, He shows us a fresh revelation of Himself, and with it, the opportunity to know a new depth of wholeness in Him.

This is not to say that we should wrap our arms around our sinfulness or just accept our excesses or insufficiencies. Hopefully by now we've established that it's good to be ruthless in ridding ourselves of any habits or ideas that keep us from holiness, freedom, health, and wholeness.

But if nothing can separate us from God's love—even though we are very much works in progress—maybe we shouldn't be so quick to turn on ourselves as we travel the messy path of healing. During such times, we need to be okay with not being okay. Unearthing is painful yet necessary. But it won't last forever.

We need Jesus every moment of every day. And wonder upon wonders, He's made Himself wholly, truly, and completely available to us in every way.

He intends to finish what He started in us. Thankfully, He's not like us in many ways. He's not motivated by appearance, achievement, accolades, or the applause of the crowd. He's not driven by ambition, insecurity, or the need to prove Himself to His critics. Though He will be phenomenally vindicated in every way on the day of His return, Jesus has no need to prove anything to anyone today. He's committed to you and me simply because He truly, profoundly loves us. And that's enough for Him.

> Jesus speaks life. He *breathes* life. When He looks at us, He sees beauty, potential, and *worth*. And He invites us to agree with Him.

Jesus wants to peel back the layers of our hearts so He can heal us deeply, profoundly, and completely. I pray you're willing to go there with me in this chapter. Because—to echo Dr. Troy's words to me—self-contempt, in any form, will do more harm to your soul and your cells than any disease ever could.

Layers of Insecurity–Phases of Holy Confidence

I've shared this story thousands of times, so if you've already heard it, please forgive me. But for the sake of the one who needs it today, I hope you'll bear with me. I battled Lyme disease as a young mom. Our finances were a wreck. I felt constantly at the mercy of others' opinions. I was self-aware in the unhealthiest way. Yet I loved Jesus. I enjoyed intimate fellowship with Him. I was saved. But I was not free.

One day I got up from my prayer time and lamented to the Lord, "Where is the victory, Lord? I pray. I fast. I memorize Scripture. I engage my faith the best way I know how. But when I get up from this place, I'm the same fearful, insecure person I've always been. Where's the victory? What am I missing?"

Jesus broke through in a whisper with words that would forever change the way I walked with Him. He whispered to my soul, *"Susie, I get that you love Me. But you don't seem to understand that I love you. So from now on, until I tell you differently, every time you want to tell Me that you love Me, I want you to turn it around and say, 'You love me, Lord.' Do it now, Susie. Say it."* So I whispered under my breath, "You love me, Lord." I sensed His nudge to say it louder with a little more gumption, so I said it louder, "You love me, Lord. In this place, amidst my mess, You love me, Lord!"

When I had a good day with the kids, I'd hear His whisper, *"Say it now."* So I'd say it, loud enough for my ears to hear it, "You love me, Lord." When I'd blow it with my kids and leave my laundry pile untouched that day, I heard the whisper, *"Say it here. Say it now."* I'd look around my little house that was falling apart—everywhere I turned I saw evidence of my not-enough-ness—but still I'd say, "Dear Jesus, You're more than enough for me. You love me, Lord, even here."

At first I wondered if this was just my own mind conjuring up ideas of self-actualization, like a self-pep talk. I wanted to find proof in Scripture that I'd indeed heard from God. Here are a couple verses that the Lord prompted me to ponder in that season of life:

> This is real love—not that we loved God, but that he loved us and sent his Son as a sacrifice to take away our sins.
>
> 1 John 4:10

> And so we know and rely on the love God has for us.
>
> 1 John 4:16 NIV

Over time, something changed deep inside me. The gap widened between how people affected me and how God affected me. Though I never thought it possible, God delivered me from the bondage of others' opinions. His opinion trumped all others because He had won my heart.

Years ago I wrote a book titled *The Uncommon Woman*, where I explored our true identity in Christ and the importance of breaking free from the bondage of others' opinions. Here's an excerpt:

> A.W. Tozer penned a compelling passage on this topic. (I reworded this quotation for women):
>
> The meek woman is not a human mouse afflicted with a sense of her own inferiority. Rather, she may be in her moral life as bold as a lion and as

strong as Samson; but she has stopped being fooled about herself. She has accepted God's estimate of her own life. She knows she is as weak and helpless as God has declared her to be, but paradoxically, she knows at the same time that she is, in the sight of God, more important than the angels. In herself, nothing, in God, everything. That is her motto. She knows well that the world will never see her as God sees her and she has stopped caring. She rests perfectly content to allow God to place His own values. She will be patient to wait for the day when everything will get its own price tag and real worth will come into its own. Then the righteous will shine forth in the kingdom of their Father. She is willing to wait for that day. In the meantime, she will have attained a place of soul rest. As she walks on in meekness, she will be happy to let God defend her. The old struggle to defend herself is over. She has found the pace that meekness brings.

Giving people easy access to dethrone our identity and devastate us is not healthy. Deep in our souls there must be an inner chamber where only Jesus resides. It's in that place where Jesus sits on the throne of our lives. By His very presence there, we are made, and continually being made whole. He has already decided our worth, so it must never be up for grabs again. Since we belong to God, we can rule in the midst of our enemies (see Psalm 110:2).[3]

For years I've walked in a freedom that I never thought possible. The more I grew in my intimacy with the Lord, the less I cared if others unfairly critiqued me. I grew to understand that Jesus doesn't miss a thing. He sees it all. An unloving word, a racial slur, or a condescending look. He notes it all. He is holy and doesn't play favorites. He will deal with my heart, and He will deal with yours. The more deeply I understood His ways, the more I concerned myself with my own motivations, thoughts, and words. If someone wanted to assess me in an ungodly, unloving way, they'd eventually have to face Jesus, and that was good enough for me.

So imagine my surprise that day in Dr. Troy's office. I didn't realize that I had new levels of insecurity to explore. Yet I've talked with many godly women who are older and wiser than I am, and all would say that their healing and wholeness process arrived in stages when they were ready for the next revelation God had for them.

Aren't the wisdom and the tenderness of God just breathtaking? He's really not in a hurry when it comes to your process. He allows it to take as long as it takes. God is the epitome of patience and kindness. I tend to believe that as long as we walk this earth, until Jesus returns, there'll be new depths of healing for our soul, next phases of wholeness to discover, and next places of promises where we can flourish—places we never imagined God had for us. We can trust where He leads and the pace with which He leads us. He's not in a hurry. So neither are we.

We don't have to go looking for the lies embedded in our souls. They'll surface in due time. We just need to do life as closely and intimately with the Savior as possible. He invites us to feast at His table, to believe His promises, and to enjoy the journey. *He opens His hands and invites us to accept ourselves and to trust Him.* And when the storms stir us up, we remember that the storms reveal the lies we believe and the truths we need.

So right in the chaos of our storm, we determine not to lose heart. We don't lose focus; we just call on the Prince of Peace. He'll either calm the storm or calm us, and then He'll show us what's true.

A Kingdom Divided

Over the years, women have rightly earned the stereotype of being petty, judgmental, and insecure. We're often so insecure about our own story that we can't resist picking apart someone else's story. But we'll never be our truest selves until we move past such childish ways. Especially in the kingdom of God. Jesus Himself said so.

> If a kingdom is divided against itself, that kingdom cannot stand. If a house is divided against itself, that house cannot stand.
>
> Mark 3:24–25 NIV

> You realize, don't you, that you are the temple of God, and God himself is present in you? No one will get by with vandalizing God's temple, you can be sure of that. God's temple is sacred—and you, remember, *are* the temple.
>
> 1 Corinthians 3:17 The Message

We can't know the damage we do to ourselves, to others, and to the greater kingdom story when we insist on believing a lie. Why do we coddle our insecurities instead of tenaciously apprehending the promises of God?

When a Christ-follower chronically wallows in insecurity and then repeatedly acts out against other women, we must know that this isn't just one of those girls-will-be-girls kinds of things. It's flat-out immaturity and sin. I've been there and done that. I've hurt women and have been hurt by women. Many years have passed since that refining time. I came through it with King David's words echoing in my ear: *It was good for me that I was afflicted. You disciplined me because I needed it. Your laws are better than life.* (See Psalm 119:71.)

I used to think that the answer for my insecurity was more compliments, accomplishments, and crowd approval. That's a lie. Those things feel good, but they don't heal us, they don't sustain us, and most important, they fail to get at the root of our need.

If we read Scripture and ponder the cross and the price Jesus paid there, and yet we still refuse to believe that we're everything to Him, I think the only answer for us is repentance. At least it was for me. I had to bow facedown and pray, "Lord, I believe. Help my unbelief. You love me, Lord. Help me to walk, talk, and live like it's true." It wasn't until I got ruthless with my insecurity and tenacious about believing that God's love and acceptance actually applied *to me*, that I started to heal from the inside out.

But something else happened along the way. Where once I cared too much about what others thought of me, I eventually died to their opinions of me, and you know how God filled those vacancies in my soul? He imparted to me a deep, profound, compassionate love for others.

Instead of walking into a room and wondering how others might size me up (that thought honestly no longer even occurs to me—praise God), I walk into a room and look for someone who needs what God has entrusted to me. I feel compassion for her struggles. I wonder what makes her thirsty. I ache for what makes her want to hide. And I want to know her story. I want her to know she's not alone. That's the kingdom way. Healing from the inside out. And it's a necessary miracle for all of us.

Dr. Troy joins me on my radio show once a month. One day before the show, we chatted about the physiological consequences of insecurity. He said the most amazing thing. "Susie, I don't think we fully comprehend how important our thought process is. Insecurity has its consequences. It fosters unhealthy thought patterns, which lead to unbelief, which then leads to poor choices—anywhere from eating terrible food to making destructive life-altering choices. But it doesn't stop there. When you harbor thoughts of insecurity, you are creating a divided kingdom within you, which cannot stand, let alone thrive. Your brain is wired to help you survive. God made it that way. So when you embrace thoughts that are contrary to life, it's like putting one foot on the gas pedal and one foot on the brake. Imagine what that would do to your motor. Your brain wants you to survive and heal and to move forward. And yet the insecure person consistently feeds the brain a contrary message. Insecurity is bad for our system. We're made for more."

Indeed, we are.

Pursue Healing ~ Pray for a Miracle
Put It into Practice

─ **Focus on . . .** ──────────────────

God's Love and How It Heals Our Hearts

─ **Scripture Says . . .** ──────────────

Love will never invoke fear. Perfect love expels fear, particularly the fear of punishment. The one who fears *punishment* has not been completed through love.

1 John 4:18 THE VOICE

I've learned of God's love with each new layer of healing He has brought into my life. Fear wrapped me in its graveclothes to such a degree that all my perceptions were skewed. But then Jesus unbound me and set me free. I've got a ways to go but there's no turning back for me. How about you? Can you picture freedom? Can you imagine enjoying the *you* God created? May He unleash over you a fresh revelation of His very personal love for you.

Science Says . . .

Fear-inducing beliefs really do damage us, and our individual beliefs are building blocks forming the ultimate picture we hold about God. The more erroneous blocks (individual doctrinal beliefs), the more distorted our picture. The greater the distortion about God, the more the activation of the brain's fear circuits, and the farther we move from God's healing plan. Yes, our beliefs about God really do matter.[4]

Pursue Healing

There's nothing like the love of God. As you draw near to Him, He *will* draw near to you. We don't overcome insecurity by trying hard not to be insecure. We overcome insecurity when we're undone by God's unfathomable love. Ask Jesus for a fresh revelation of how He feels about you. Ask Him why He made you. Ask Him to speak to you about your insecurities. Remind your soul daily that you are already seated with Him, already victorious because of Him, already secure in Him.

Pray for a Miracle

Jesus, I ask You to do a miracle in me! Unearth every shred of insecurity and fill those vacancies with more of Your love. Show me the lies I picked up when life let me down. I open my hands and lift my eyes and say with all my heart, have Your way in me! Help me to live a life totally disproportionate to who I am! Uproot every lie and plant new seeds of truth. I long to be a living, breathing miracle; a trophy of grace; a testament of Your redeeming power. My soul waits for You! Amen.

Soul Searching

In what ways has God delivered you from insecurity? How has insecurity surfaced for you in this particular season of life?

_____

_____

_____

_____

_____

_____

_____

> Father in heaven, I thank You for being my Great Defender. You defend and deliver me not because I am perfect but because You are. I am an heir of God, a joint heir with Christ. As part of my inheritance, I am privileged to be seated with You, hidden in You, and protected by You. This means that NO weapon formed against me will prosper. And anyone who rises up to take me out will not succeed. You will deal with my critics and You will defend my honor. I don't have to fear man because I live to honor You. Thank you, Lord. My soul trusts in You!
>
> Isaiah 54:17 (paraphrase)

Prayer

Precious Lord, thank You for loving me like You do! Thank You for Your patience with me. Thank You for defending my honor and for delivering me from the hands of my enemy. I have every reason to walk with holy confidence and humble dependence. Forgive me for clinging to my insecurities more than I cling to Your promises. Fill me with holy boldness this hour! Rise up within me and make me mighty in battle, powerful in speech, tenacious in prayer. I am done with low thinking and low talking. Heal me in the depths of my being so I can love well and live with a whole heart. I will rise up to take my place with You, Lord. Fill me afresh with the sense of Your great love; help me to flourish in it and live like it's true. Pour out a tangible sense of Your Spirit on me and through me so that everyone I meet may hunger to know You more. I am forever Yours and forever grateful. Thank You, Lord. In Jesus' name I pray. Amen.

Life Reflection

1. There seem to be two extremes when it comes to how we treat ourselves: Either we struggle to offer self-compassion to our souls because we're so aware of our failures (we make more of our sin than we do of our Savior), or we're too quick to let ourselves off the hook because we skim over they ways we sin (we make light of our sin and of our desperate need for a Savior). Be as honest as you're able. Which extreme do you bend toward? How does your mindset affect your intimacy with God?

2. How would you define insecurity? Why does this issue plague us so? Write down your thoughts.

3. Think back to your earliest memory of insecurity—the first time self-doubt entered your story. Write down that memory and how you felt.

4. Pause here and spend some time with Jesus. Picture Him in the Gospels. Put your story in one of those scenes. Imagine Him approaching you on His way to meet the woman at the well. What do you imagine He'd say to you, do for you? Write down your thoughts.

5. Prayerfully ask Jesus to show you how He sees you. Wait and listen. Read more of the Gospels. When you're ready, write a listening prayer (in His voice to you). Some will balk at this exercise, but I ask you to try it. You're not writing Scripture—it's already been written. But Jesus Himself said we'd know His voice; we'd know what He sounds like. Scripture also tells us that we know only in part. So we're not going to get it right all the time. Even so, consider this a listening prayer exercise. How do you suppose Jesus feels about you? Wait and listen. Then put pen to paper.

Spiritual Reset

PRAISE

All those decisions your family misinterpreted and the accusations you bore, the many ways you paid for it. The thousands of unseen choices to overlook a cutting remark, a failure, to be kind to that friend who failed you again. The things that you wish you had personally done better, but at the time no one knew what you were laboring under—the warfare, the depression, the chronic fatigue. The millions of ways you have been missed and terribly misunderstood. Your Defender will make it all perfectly clear; you will be vindicated.[5]

PRAISE—Acronym Exercise

P—Praise Him. Write out a prayer of thanksgiving just because He is God.

_____

_____

_____

R—Remember and Repent. Write out a memory of God's faithfulness. Spend time with Him and repent of anything He brings to mind.

_____

_____

_____

A—Ask Him for what's on your heart.

_____

_____

_____

I—Intercede for others.

_____

_____

_____

S—Stand on God's promises. Write out a promise that under-girds what you're asking Him for.

_____

_____

_____

E—Eternity. Put your life, your burdens, and your prayer list up to the lens of eternity. Ask Jesus to help you look up and think long, with eternity in mind.

_____

_____

_____

Digging Deeper

*Use a journal or notebook for this section.

A. Read Galatians 2:20 and rewrite it in your own words. But first take some time to ponder what it means that your sin, your deficiencies, your self-contempt, your insecurity have all been nailed to the cross. Imagine these as parasites swimming around in your body, draining life from your system. Then picture yourself making the Galatians 2:20 faith declaration over your life. By Christ's victory and on His authority, these things have to cease and desist; they have to die because Jesus now lives in you! Imagine them as they shrivel up, die off, and disappear. Now, with as much boldness as you can muster, write out your own Galatians 2:20 faith declaration.

B. Read John 1:12 in several translations, if you're able. You'll notice the interchangeable words *right* and *power*. This word translates this way: delegated power and influence. God Most High has delegated authority and influence to everyone who calls on the name of Jesus for salvation. To the extent that we walk in it, we will increase in it. God has imparted good gifts to us. He's put His Spirit in us. He's written promises over us. We have everything we need to walk our journey with precision and power, faith, hope, and love. Unfortunately, our own negative thought patterns and unhealthy habits keep us from the best of what God has for us. What thought patterns have kept you from rightly stewarding your God-given influence?

C. Read Ephesians 2:10 and consider this truth: You are God's poetry. His work of art. He created you masterfully and intends to use you powerfully. Look ahead to a year from now. What would an upgrade in holy confidence look like for you? And what would you love to accomplish *with* God and *for* Him? Give some thought to these answers.

D. Read Ephesians 1:3 and write out a bold prayer asking God to show you, in tangible ways, what this means for you. Ask Him for a greater capacity to understand this truth. Ask Him what obedience looks like for you in this particular season of life.

E. Revisit the passages above—Galatians 2:20; John 1:12; Ephesians 2:10; and Ephesians 1:3—and write out four bold, concise faith statements on a postcard and make an extra copy. Tuck one in your Bible, put the other one where you spend a lot of time. Several times a day say your faith statements out loud. Let your ears hear your mouth declare God's truth over your life. It'll change your neural pathways, your physiology, your heart, and your perspective. I'm excited for you to do this exercise. It'll shoot adrenaline into your soul!

> **Find the following downloadable print at SusieLarson.com.**

I am PROFOUNDLY *LOVED*,
DIVINELY *EQUIPPED*,
IRREVOCABLY *ACCEPTED*...

I REFUSE INSECURITY.

I REJECT INFERIORITY.

I EMBRACE MY AUTHORITY

BECAUSE I AM SEATED WITH CHRIST.

I have a place at the table of grace.

nine

I'm Selfish

Jesus, Make Me Brave!

We love because he first loved us.

1 John 4:19 NIV

Although at times God heals us instantaneously, most times healing happens as we practice loving interactions with God and His people.[1]

ONE OF THE GREATEST FLAWS IN MY CHARACTER, the thing God has had to address in me over and over again, layer by layer, has been my bent toward self-preservation. For much of my life, I've been motivated by fear. As God peeled back the layers of my fear, I've had to look at my instinctive, selfish tendency to self-protect. I've hurt people I love with this fear reaction. I've missed out on certain faith adventures because of self-preservation. My fear had made me selfish.

Dying to self has called me to hang in there and have the difficult conversations when my flesh made me want to run and hide. Dying to self compelled me to reach out and encourage the abundantly blessed when I myself felt marginalized. Dying to self compelled me to travel to a third-world country to see firsthand the work of International Justice Mission right in the midst of a full speaking season, struggling health, and huge fears around international travel. Dying to self compels me to take risks with my story knowing that it's fodder for the gossips, in hopes that I can help even one.

I've learned that every time I die to my self-life, resurrection power waits for me on the other side. There's no death I can die that won't be met by God's overwhelming compassion, power, and goodness.

> Precious in the sight of the Lord
> is the death of his faithful servants.
> Psalm 116:15 NIV

I'm quite sure the psalmist meant the literal death of God's people, but I think it's biblically sound to say that Jesus is profoundly moved *any* time we die a flesh-death so we can more wholeheartedly live for Him.

I'm no longer afraid to die to the parts of me that need to go. God has shown me again and again that to live is Christ and to die is gain.[2]

It's true that the flesh dies hard, but it's a small death compared to the robust life that awaits us on the other side of our obedience.

Believe it or not, the unhealed places in our hearts make us either selfish or self-sacrificing, both of which have an unhealthy element of self in them.

> The unhealed places in our hearts make us either selfish or *self-sacrificing*, both of which have an unhealthy element of self in them.

I once knew a servant-hearted girl who refused help from others. She always gave. Was always tired. Consistently ministered. But rarely let anyone in on her story. Everyone was in debt to her. But nobody really knew her.

I once knew an introvert who took her need for solitude to an absolute extreme. She reasoned that since people and plans exhausted her, her sole purpose on earth was to make sure she protected her space. Hers was a very small life.

I once knew a wealthy woman who generously gave gifts to many. Often with strings attached. She stayed in the center of her universe and managed things on her terms. Her space was unsafe for most everybody but her.

I once knew a woman who prided herself on her simple ways. She didn't overindulge or live with excess. Yet her continual *simple* requests made her impossible to please. Since she asked for so little, she expected to receive exactly what she asked for, no matter if her unreasonable demands cost others time and money. Her self-focused life was obvious to everyone but her.

I have a friend who consistently overbooked his schedule. He was exhausted, weary, and in need of a fresh touch from God. Someone told him about a therapy retreat where he could get some rest but also receive direction on what persistently drove him. One day during a group session, the instructor offered this scenario to the group and asked for input: They were all on a sinking ship. Not enough lifeboats to go around. How do you respond?

My friend raised his tired hand and said, "I'd give up my place in the lifeboat." The instructor turned on a dime and said, "You would, would you? Why is that?" My friend replied, "Because I care about people and can't bear the thought of taking somebody else's place."

That's exactly the kind of guy he is. He's one of my favorite people on the planet. He thought for sure the instructor would appreciate his sincere answer. He'd often received affirmation for the many ways he gave of himself to others. But he didn't expect what came next.

The instructor stepped in a little closer and said, "I'd suggest that you're willing to give up your lifeboat for a totally different reason."

My friend's eyebrows arched. He sat up a little straighter and suddenly felt a bit uncomfortable in that setting.

The instructor continued, "I don't believe you answered the way you did because you're unselfish. You may be an unselfish person in general, but I don't believe that's what motivates you in this case. I think the reason you're willing to give up your place on the lifeboat is because you don't value your life at all. You've been running on empty without healthy boundaries for a long time. It's not too difficult to throw away something you don't value. How do you suppose that mindset affects your wife and children?"

That was a breakthrough moment for my friend.

Self-preservation and unhealthy self-sacrifice have many faces. We can spot it in others and totally miss it in ourselves.

The Hero in All of Us

Selfishness kills the hero in all of us. Consider King Saul. He was God's answer to the laments of God's people. He was a tall, handsome warrior. And completely insecure. Saul experienced a miraculous, prophetic encounter with the prophet Samuel. God confirmed Saul's calling exactly as Samuel predicted, and God poured out His Spirit on Saul in a way that tangibly touched him from the inside out. Wouldn't it be amazing to receive so many confirmations on your calling?

Yet when the time came for Saul to be acclaimed as king, when the people were ready to acknowledge their God-given leader, he was nowhere to be seen. They found him hiding in the baggage. His first act as king was all about him and not at all about the people.

Before we judge him too harshly, we might need to take inventory of our own lives. How many times have we hidden in, behind, or because of our own baggage? We're pretty savvy when it comes to avoiding scenarios that make us feel small, out of our element, or in need of recognition. We hide in our busyness, we hide in our comforts, and we even hide behind our Christian activity. We all do.

> The more we *heal*, the less we tend to hide. . . . We're our *best* selves when we're whole. We love others *better* when our hearts are healed.

But one thing I know: The more we heal, the less we tend to hide. This is why God invites us to earnestly pursue healing *and* pray for a miracle. We're our best selves when we're whole. We love others better when our hearts are healed.

God would have done so much more in, through, and for Saul if Saul had dealt as ruthlessly with his insecurities as he did with David, the object of his jealousy. Instead of dying to self and living for God, Saul thought that he could kill David and take what he wanted from God. But it doesn't work that way.

Like a leaf tossed about by the wind, Saul vacillated between his feelings and his convictions. Everything he said and did was selfish because he was worried about himself. . . . Although Saul had been called by God and had a mission in life, he struggled constantly with jealousy, insecurity, arrogance, impulsiveness, and deceit. He did not decide to be wholeheartedly committed to God. *Because Saul would not let God's love give rest to his heart, he never became God's man.*[3]

Imagine how much of our angst would dissipate if we allowed God's love to bring rest to our hearts. Joy, peace, and rest would replace jealousy, striving, and comparing.

So how do we discern between selfishness and wisdom when it comes to our schedule and the way we live? Jesus taught that things are proven right by their fruit. What may be obedience for one might be self-preservation for another. And people will always have opinions about how you and I manage our schedule, time, treasures, and talents.

I'm passionate about this topic because one day we'll each give an account for how we stewarded the opportunities God afforded us. It matters not only what we do but also *why* we do it. I wrote a whole book on the idea of breaking free from the rat race and from the bondage of others' opinions so we can run the sacred race. It's called *Your Sacred Yes: Trading Life-Draining Obligation for Freedom, Passion, and Joy.* That book was born out of fifteen years of tried and tested abiding life principles. I pray you'll have the chance to read it someday.

So for now, I want to set aside that part of the conversation. Let's look at a different aspect of our self-life that we might normally miss.

Last chapter we talked about the importance of self-love and self-compassion. We cannot heal until we become a friend to our own soul. Remember? A kingdom divided cannot stand. God Himself charged us to love Him and love others as we love ourselves.

"Love the Lord your God with all your heart and with all your soul and with all your mind and with all your strength." The second is this: "Love your neighbor as yourself." There is no commandment greater than these.

Mark 12:30–31 NIV

The word *love* used twice in this passage, translates *agape* this way: Agape—

- To welcome
- To entertain
- To be fond of
- To love dearly
- To be well pleased
- To be well contented with[4]

Do we love God this way? Do we love our neighbor this way? Do we imagine that God loves us this way? Do we love *ourselves* this way?

Why would we offer Him something we don't think twice about, merely tolerate, or worse yet, despise? And how does laying down our lives connect to living the *fully alive* life He offers us?

> Then Jesus said to his disciples, "Whoever wants to be my disciple must deny themselves and take up their cross and follow me. For whoever wants to save their life will lose it, but whoever loses their life for me will find it. What good will it be for someone to gain the whole world, yet forfeit their soul? Or what can anyone give in exchange for their soul? For the Son of Man is going to come in his Father's glory with his angels, and then he will reward each person according to what they have done.
>
> Matthew 16:24–27 NIV

So many of these kingdom concepts are mysterious and not easily discerned without God's help. Yet as we follow Him and trust Him and die to the very things that are harmful to our souls, we find life bursting in us, we become who we never thought we could be, and we know—on a deeper level—that what God says is true!

When we receive a fresh revelation of God's love for us, we will walk in a renewed love for others. When we start to grasp the immense value of our soul, we will contend for the freedoms Christ won for us. When we see the importance of our presence on this earth, we'll be more apt to fight the good fight of faith so that others might win too.

I mentioned this in the last chapter, but it bears repeating: Insecurity is just another form of selfishness. If I don't ever grasp who I am in Christ, I'll live most of my life with me in mind.

One day while spending some time with the Lord around this idea, I asked Him to show me what symptoms I should watch for—evidence in my life that I'm living for me, not for Him. He gave me three words—and I think these are signs and symptoms for all of us that indicate we've forgotten who we are:

- Pity
- Proof
- Praise

When we say and do things so that others feel sorry for us, we've forgotten who we are. When we misuse our time, treasure, and talents to prove something Jesus has already proven, we've forgotten who we are. And when we strive for the praise of man and forget about the praise of God, we've simply forgotten who we are.

Any time we posture for position or accolades from man, we do so with a heart of unbelief. And we miss out on the honor that comes from God alone. Jesus said so Himself:

> No wonder you can't believe! For you gladly honor each other, but you don't care about the honor that comes from the one who alone is God.
>
> John 5:44

We don't need *pity* because we have the promises of God! There's a place for lament and grief, yes. But when our thought pattern morphs into self-pity, we've stopped thinking like heirs. Anything born out of our flesh will be terrible for our soul, bad for our health, and damaging to our relationships.

Flesh gives birth to flesh, but the Spirit gives birth to spirit.

John 3:6 NIV

If the enemy is tempting you toward self-pity, it's because he wants you living out of your flesh instead of walking by the Spirit. He wants you looking down when you should be looking up. He wants you looking inward when God calls you to look upward. And he wants you nursing your wounds in an unhealthy way when God would have you grab hold of His promises in the most valiant way. You are an heir. Never forget it.

We don't need to *prove* anything to anybody. Jesus set us free to live for Him! He'll always be our advocate, our defender, and our deliverer.

If you're tempted to expend precious, valuable energy to prove to someone that you're really something, I challenge you, dear friend, to humbly entrust your whole identity to God instead. Stop your striving and seek to know God more intimately in this place (see Psalm 46:10). God issues you a beautiful invitation to trust Him more fully with your value, your calling, and even your reputation. He can establish you in a moment's time. If He has you hidden for now, trust His Fatherly protection and His wise preparation.

And finally, though we all love to be noticed, affirmed, and recognized on occasion (nothing wrong with that), we don't need the *praise* of man to be okay. When we catch ourselves playing to the crowd for the applause, death-to-self invites us to die to our desperate need for validation and to turn our hearts toward Jesus. Our goal isn't to be loved (we're already loved, and not because we've earned it); our goal is to love and honor and worship God.

The next time you catch yourself looking for praise in all the wrong places, turn up the worship music and *give Him praise*. Perspective returns when we put God in His rightful place. Worship brings our heart back into rhythm with God's heart. He's the one who restores our soul.

We Will Overcome

We live in a selfish world. It's in our nature to think of ourselves. Apart from Christ's work in us, we will bend toward our own brand of selfishness, which will always cost us, our calling, and those God has given us to love. Selfishness even negatively impacts our health. And God has made us for so much more! What are the physiological consequences of putting ourselves at the center of our universe?

Most recently, a new study of the genetic effects of happiness found that humans are rewarded with healthy gene activity when we are unselfish, and we are punished—at a basic microscopic, cellular level—when we put our own needs first. To reach this conclusion, researchers from the University of North Carolina and the University of California, Los Angeles, had eighty healthy volunteers complete an online questionnaire that asked why they felt satisfied with their lives. Then the researchers drew their blood and analyzed their white blood cells to see their "gene expression," a complex process by which genes direct the production of proteins that control immune response. People whose happiness was based on a sense of higher purpose and service to others had gene markers indicating low levels of inflammation, which has been linked to the development of cancer and heart disease. By the same token, people whose happiness was based on material things and servicing their own needs first had gene markers indicating poorer immune response and greater vulnerability to infection. They appeared to be at increased risk of cancer, diabetes, and cardiovascular disease.[5]

Isn't it something to watch science catch up with Scripture? We know that unselfishness is good for our communities and good for our souls. We know that something powerful happens when we love others as Christ has loved us. But now scientists are verifying this truth: *God's Word and God's ways affect us on a cellular level.* Doesn't that just boggle the mind?

Scripture also tells us that there will come a day when lawlessness increases and the love of most grows cold. My mentor said recently, "I think it'll be the 'lawful' who will be most offended and impacted by these evil days. Those who want lawlessness are getting what they want." In other words, we will have plenty of opportunities to be offended, put out, and shoved aside.

What will we do? How will we respond? How will we keep from becoming reactionary, selfish people like the masses we see on the news? How will we overcome?

I'm Selfish

Is it possible to live *fully alive* in a culture that seems to be dying before our very eyes?

> And they overcame and conquered him because of the blood of the Lamb and because of the word of their testimony, for they did not love their life and renounce their faith even when faced with death.
>
> Revelation 12:11 AMP

We overcome by the blood of the Lamb, by the word of our testimony, and we love not our lives, even unto death.

Can you see why the enemy would want to bait us into pity, proof, and praise? If we're feeling sorry for ourselves, we'll be thinking only about ourselves. If we're trying to prove we're something, we'll focus on our measly efforts and not on Christ's awesome, overwhelming victory on the cross. We need *power* to stand in these latter days.

The Blood

We overcome by the potent, powerful, shed blood of our Lord Jesus Christ. Not by fancy schemes, clever formulas, or popular methods. The blood of Jesus will never lose its power. His blood saves us, heals us, and redeems us. His royal blood runs through our veins. To be under the blood is to be ultimately delivered from sin and death. What are the benefits for those who are under the blood?

> Praise the Lord, my soul;
>   all my inmost being, praise his holy name.
> Praise the Lord, my soul,
>   and forget not all his benefits—
> who forgives all your sins
>   and heals all your diseases,
> who redeems your life from the pit
>   and crowns you with love and compassion,
> who satisfies your desires with good things
>   so that your youth is renewed like the eagle's.
>
> Psalm 103:1–5 NIV

What if you spent some time praying through that passage *on a regular basis*? What if your brain became familiarized with these truths to such a degree that they changed your physiology? What if your body, mind, and spirit suddenly grasped—on a cellular level—how loved and forgiven you are? And what if you lived with a brand-new expectancy regarding

- God's desire to heal you
- His intention to bless you
- His desire to satisfy your desires with *good things*?

I pray this prayer regularly, and it's better than any vitamin supplement I can find on the market. This passage reminds me that God so loves and values my life that I can turn around and love others as He has loved me. I lose nothing when I lay down my selfish ways, and I gain a knowledge of Christ, an experience with Him that is utterly priceless to me.

Our Testimony

We overcome by the blood of the Lamb and the *word* of our testimony, which translates as a word, decree, or mandate given by God Himself. How often do our words reflect God's mandates and decrees over our lives?

Might we need an upgrade on how we speak about our trials and tribulations? I know I sure did. Once I started to pay attention to my laments, I realized how often I talked myself into a faithless, unbelieving rut.

Our testimony must testify to the promises and faithfulness of God—even in our not-yet seasons. He speaks His decrees over our lives, we walk in them, they change us (and our circumstances), and suddenly, our testimony becomes an encouragement to others, a trophy of God's grace, and a weapon in spiritual warfare.

Brave Love

We overcome by the blood of the Lamb and the word of our testimony, and we *love not* our lives, even unto death.

I had to scratch my head for a moment when I realized that the word *love* in Revelation 12:11 is the same word used in Mark 12:31: *agape.*

So how do we wholeheartedly love ourselves and yet love not ourselves, even unto death?

To deny ourselves before we value ourselves is not much of an offering to God. But when you've contended for the promises of God in your life, when you've stood strong against the enemy and refused to let him bait you into sin or steal what God has promised you, when you've persevered in battle and have been trained by your trials . . . well then, you understand a little better the significance of your life. You have a firmer grasp on the value of your soul, the power of God's promises, and the importance of your call.

> To deny ourselves before we *value* ourselves is not much of an *offering* to God.

In fact, have you noticed? The longer you walk with Him, the more you anticipate eternity with God. You realize that life on earth is short and eternity is long. And though God gives us good gifts and lots of grace for this journey, we'll see some of our greatest treasures and breakthroughs on the other side.

To walk intimately with God, to stand strong in battle, and to trust Him with our not-yets turns us into warriors. And along the way, we develop enough of a history with God to know that we also have a profound future awaiting us with Him.

We're willing to continue on, to march, believe, and trust.

As we grow, we realize that our lives have unfathomable value—that nothing can separate us from our Father in heaven who loves us. No enemy can snatch us out of His hand. No demon can derail our calling. And no jealous, petty person can gossip enough to God to make Him change His mind about us. Unfathomable, yes?

As you and I grow in our identity, we become more secure about eternity. We value our life and our call, but we value Jesus more. We follow His lead. He did not consider *equality with God* a thing to leverage or grasp or to parade in front of those who didn't acknowledge Him. He was content to be misunderstood because He came for those who knew they needed Him.

This passage takes my breath away. Read it out loud if you can:

Don't be selfish; don't try to impress others. Be humble, thinking of others as better than yourselves. Don't look out only for your own interests, but take an interest in others, too.

You must have the same attitude that Christ Jesus had.

Though he was God,
> he did not think of equality with God
> as something to cling to.
Instead, he gave up his divine privileges
> he took the humble position of a slave
> and was born as a human being.
When he appeared in human form,
> he humbled himself in obedience to God
> and died a criminal's death on a cross.

Therefore, God elevated him to the place of highest honor
> and gave him the name above all other names,
that at the name of Jesus every knee should bow,
> in heaven and on earth and under the earth,
and every tongue declare that Jesus Christ is Lord,
> to the glory of God the Father.

Philippians 2:3–11

I once read a story about a mother of sons. I'm a mother of sons. But two of her sons were beheaded on the same day. They were among the twenty-one Coptic Christians beheaded by ISIS. They refused to deny Jesus, even in the face of death. They loved not their lives, even unto death. I read about how this dear mother, right in the midst of her grief, shared that if those who killed her sons returned to their village, she would invite them in for a meal, just for one more chance to share the love of Jesus with them.

That mother is an overcomer. *Oh, to know the love of Christ in such a way!*

How will we stand in these trying times? How can we shine brightly and bravely in this ever-darkening world? How will we know wholeness and health in a world that's got a terminal illness?

We walk intimately with our Savior. We focus more on His promise than on our problems. We rehearse His goodness and remember His faithfulness.

When people come against us and we're tempted to return the favor, we return a blessing instead. When people selfishly grab what belonged to us, we bow low, open our hands, and entrust our whole soul to Jesus once again. When someone steps in front of us in line, we smile and thank God for a chance to practice grace.

In the days ahead, we'll be given plenty of opportunities to humble ourselves, die to ourselves. May we take every single one of them. We can do so joyfully because we know that every death will be swallowed up in victory. Every injustice will be accounted for. Every offering multiplied. And every wound healed.

We serve a risen Savior. He's coming again. He will reward and vindicate His people. He will judge and convict His enemies. And He *will* make all things new.

Pursue Healing ~ Pray for a Miracle
Put It into Practice

Focus on . . .

Your God-Shaped Heart

Scripture Says . . .

For now, we can only see a dim and blurry picture of things, as when we stare into polished metal. I realize that everything I know is only part of the big picture. But one day, when Jesus arrives, we will see clearly, face-to-face. In that day, I will fully know just as I have been wholly known by God. But now faith, hope, and love remain; these three virtues must characterize our lives. The greatest of these is love.

1 Corinthians 13:12–13 The Voice

When we reach the limits of our love, when our selfishness surfaces, and when we're tempted toward self-contempt, it's the perfect time to remember God's love. Ponder His love for you. Imagine the smile on His eyes when He looks at you. Instead of trying to make your own heart good, thank Him for the supernatural miracle at work within you even now. He's up to something good in you.

Science Says . . .

A corruption in our thinking can and does cause negative changes in the brain and body. Unhealthy thought patterns activate the brain's stress circuits causing inflammatory cascades that, if not resolved, damage insulin receptors and increase the risk for diabetes mellitus type II, heart attacks, strokes, obesity, high cholesterol, depression, dementia, and other health problems.[6]

Pursue Healing

Dare to ask God this question (on a regular basis):

In what ways do I think wrongly about You, Lord? Show me what's true.

Be more tenacious about guarding your heart from every thought that weakens you and every attitude that poisons you.

Fill your heart and mind with thoughts of God's grand involvement in your life.

Pray for a Miracle

Heavenly Father, I long to be more like You! Thank You for Your unending commitment to my transformation. I'm asking for a tangible, life-changing miracle in my heart. Meet me here, in this place, and give me a revelation of Your love for me. Pour out Your Spirit upon me so that I see others like You do. Put passion in my heart so I will step out and tend to the concerns on Your heart. I know I'm asking for something that You want to do for me, so I will wait in full faith for my miracle. In Jesus' name I pray. Amen.

Soul Searching

Do you bend toward self-protection or unhealthy self-sacrifice?

_____

_____

_____

_____

_____

Heavenly Father, I ask You, by the power of Your Holy Spirit to infuse me with a fresh revelation of Your love. I don't just want to pretend to love others, I want to really, truly love them with courage, compassion, conviction, and genuine affection. I want to walk in such a holy confidence that I find it easy and joyful to honor others in my presence. I want to be so aware of how rich I am in You that I live with an open hand to help those in need. May I be so filled with Your Spirit that I instinctively bless those who curse me. Help me walk in step with those who celebrate and with those who suffer. I humble myself and confess that I don't know half of what I think I do! I will walk humbly with a teachable spirit. I'll enjoy the company of ordinary people, and marvel that You keep company with me. Help me to reflect Your heart to live in peace with others as far as it concerns me. Amen.

Romans 12:9–16 (paraphrase)

Prayer

Precious Father, I humble myself before You today. I bow low, open my hands, and confess my tendency to save myself, preserve myself, and/or dismiss myself. You've made me in Your image. I am fearfully and wonderfully made. Since I belong to You, I belong. I'm not an outcast and never will be. I cannot fathom my value and I cannot comprehend the price You paid to grant me a seat at the table of grace.

Forgive me for the countless ways I try to take my life into my own hands. Help me to live by the Spirit so I won't gratify my flesh's desire to live and control what You've already purchased. Give me a fresh vision of what Your love could look like in me and through me. Deliver me from the bondage of others' opinions so I can live and serve with a free and whole heart. Help me to remember that my stewardship before You may at times look like selfishness to others. Grant me an increased capacity to imagine what's possible when I surrender it all to You. Keep me close to Your heartbeat even though I'm prone to wander. Heal the deepest parts of me so I can love others in a way that helps them heal.

You've made me to be an overcomer. Help me to know the power of Your blood, to appropriate the word of my testimony, and to love You more than I love my own life. Grant me the courage to lay it down in whatever ways You ask of me. I'm living with eternity in mind. Help me to finish strong, Lord. In Your mighty name I pray, amen.

Life Reflection

1. Revisit the scenarios described at the beginning of the chapter. Which one most resonates with you? Write down your thoughts.

2. Not one of us is too messy for God. He works wonders in the worst situations! So what was it about Saul's story that thwarted God's best plan for him? Read 1 Samuel 9–11 to get more context.

3. How have your own sins kept you from the best of what God has for you? (I know this is a tough question, but do know you are not alone! It takes great courage to do this kind of work. God has more for you.)

4. In what ways have you gained ground? How has the Holy Spirit lifted you out of your self-tendencies to become more like Christ?

5. What area of your life is God putting His finger on these days? Remember, His voice is gentle and life-affirming.

Spiritual Reset

I wake up my spirit to the creative power of God by reminding myself of what He has already done, I have faith to face whatever this battle brings. I am sometimes tempted to move into the ditch of self-pity and despair and stay there, but I don't because I know He has created me for more. I want to live wonderstruck by His power and skill. Our God is a creative genius, and we are His best work. It's a wonder too great for words.[7]

PRAISE—Acronym Exercise

P—Praise Him. Write out a prayer of thanksgiving just because He is God.

_____

_____

_____

R—Remember and Repent. Write out a memory of God's faithfulness. Spend time with Him and repent of anything He brings to mind.

_____

_____

_____

A—Ask Him for what's on your heart.

_____

_____

_____

I—Intercede for others.

_____

_____

_____

S—Stand on God's promises. Write out a promise that under-girds what you're asking Him for.

_____

_____

_____

E—Eternity. Put your life, your burdens, and your prayer list up to the lens of eternity. Ask Jesus to help you look up and think long, with eternity in mind.

_____

_____

_____

Digging Deeper

*Use your journal or notebook for this section.

A. Read Romans 12:1–2 and prayerfully ask the Lord what your offering might look like in this particular season of life. Also, ask God to show you the value of your precious offering. Your life matters deeply to Him. Write down your thoughts.

B. Read Galatians 2:20 and write it out in a personalized way. List some of the things you want to die to (sin, sickness, addiction, excess, self-protection, etc.).

C. Read Romans 8:5–11 and notice how connected our thought-life is to whether we walk in the Spirit or in the flesh. We want *life* and we want *peace*. This passage tells us how to have both. Take some time to prayerfully ponder this passage. Ask God to search your heart and show what it would look like for you to walk more consistently by the Spirit working mightily within you.

D. Let's visit Romans 12 again. This time read the whole chapter and make note of every instance that speaks of dying to self. In other words, in what ways does this passage call us to live in an other-worldly way? Write down every example. Then write out your own personalized prayer.

> Find the following downloadable print
> at SusieLarson.com.

I value my life

BECAUSE JESUS DOES.

I steward my gifts

BECAUSE JESUS ASKED ME TO.

I believe for miracles

BECAUSE JESUS LIVES IN ME.

I lay down my life

BECAUSE JESUS WILL RAISE ME UP AGAIN.

He Rewards

Receive It

> No eye has seen, no ear has heard, and no mind has imagined what God has prepared for those who love him.
>
> 1 Corinthians 2:9

Consider what rediscovering the connection between your life now and your life in eternity could mean for you. If your actions today do have the potential to radically affect your eternity, wouldn't that dramatically change how you think about your life? How you think about God? What you choose to do one minute from now?[1]

HERE I STAND, at the edge of my promised land.

I wiggle my toes in the soft green grass and I survey the scene before me. Where once I saw thorns and thickets, new life abounds.

My once-fallow ground *was* hallowed ground, just like the Lord had said. And now I see a fruitful field.

I remember the season when the soil and rocks were overturned, the ground unearthed, and the weeds utterly exposed. I remember how it looked. I remember how it felt. I wondered if I'd always feel that way.

But now? This new territory is fertile, fruitful, and lush. Beautiful to the discerning eye.

I'm in awe of what God has done.

> You drench the plowed ground with rain,
>   melting the clods and leveling the ridges.
> You soften the earth with showers
>   and bless its abundant crops.
> You crown the year with a bountiful harvest;
>   even the hard pathways overflow with abundance.
> The grasslands of the wilderness become a lush pasture,
>   and the hillsides blossom with joy.
> The meadows are clothed with flocks of sheep,
>   and the valleys are carpeted with grain.
>   They all shout and sing for joy!
>
> Psalm 65:10–13

I look across the landscape and remember the times I tried to occupy this land, land that God had promised me. The enemy seemed to own it. And every time I'd try to lay hold of my promised place, he'd get loud and throw dirt in my eyes. Feisty as I am, I couldn't seem to win against him. Time and time again I'd retreat within the boundaries of my known zone, frustrated that I could not seem to win the fear-worry-sickness battle. Sometimes I'd gain inches but never the land.

But then the storm hit. The winds howled. The elements raged. And the enemy spewed his threats with increased fervency. He had me in his crosshairs. He seemed to have a renewed resolve to take me out.

I felt sure that *this* storm would be the end of me.

One day while hiding in my own cave of self-protection, I remembered reading in the Old Testament about how Saul and David were at odds. Okay, maybe that's an understatement. Saul actually wanted to kill David because he was jealous of and threatened by him.

He Rewards

Saul seemed to have the advantage because of his position and possessions, yet it was David who grew stronger in battle. Saul grew weaker over time. David gained strength in the fight because God was with him.

I knew I was on the winning side. I learned that the enemy doesn't have endless strength. I learned that worship on the battlefield is really the most powerful form of spiritual warfare. I realized that my heart for Jesus and His heart for me would be the devil's undoing.

Like David, my enemy was jealous of me. I threatened him. Why? I have the Spirit of the living God mightily at work within me. I am the object of the Father's love. I have the armies of heaven cheering me on. There's absolutely nothing the enemy can do to take away my firm place in the Father's heart or to diminish my firm standing in His kingdom.

The devil can stir up trouble, he can stir up my fears, but he can't touch my soul. He can't ruin my future.

So this time, amidst this storm, Jesus urged me onward. This time I was ready to face my fears and take my land. This time was my time. And this land was mine.

> A little while, and the wicked will be no more;
>> though you look for them, they will not be found.
> But the meek will inherit the land
>> and enjoy peace and prosperity.
>
> Psalm 37:10–11 NIV

I stand on the edges of this land and marvel. I'm not who I was before this storm. I don't have the fear I once had. I don't catastrophize when symptoms flare or when the ground shakes. I know—on a deeper level—what's true about God.

I'm healthier than I once was. I have more clarity now than I did before. And I'm wiser to the enemy's schemes.

For me to steward the territory before me, I needed to up my game. It didn't matter if others seemed to get away with looser boundaries. God's invitation to me is unique to me, just as your call and your journey of obedience will be quite unique to you.

Jesus was calling me upward and onward, and I intended to follow Him. I was determined to stay on His heels.

Over the years I'd worked hard on renewing my mind, but I had no idea how much I needed to grow in this area. I thought I knew how to worship in battle, feast on the battlefield, and pray like my life depended upon it, but I didn't know what I didn't know.

I thought I ate healthy foods, but I learned that in order to fight my particular health battle, but I needed to eat even healthier foods. I figured I'd always be someone who would struggle with insomnia. But I decided to go after it because sleep is *critical* to good health, mind, body, and spirit. And besides, God grants sleep to those He loves.[2] I know He loves me. Now I not only sleep at night, I dream. Imagine.

With God's grace I confronted one self-limiting belief after another. I broke through an invisible barrier that I had accepted for far too long. Once God upgraded my vision for what was possible in Him, I took the next steps He put in front of me.

The physical and emotional adjustments and tweaks I've made over the past two years required focus, discipline, and persistence. But now they're paying me back in dividends. But there's more to this land than meets the eye.

> Physical training is good, but training for godliness is much better, promising benefits in this life and in the life to come.
>
> 1 Timothy 4:8

Our battles give us an opportunity for faith. And our faith has eternal consequences. What we possess of God's kingdom here determines how we live in His kingdom there, in eternity with Him. For now, we have to contend for some of the things God has promised us. Yet there's a treasure hidden within every trial.

The land before us is a good land. There'll be giants to conquer, battles to face, and maturity to gain, but we have what we need to make the journey and take the territory before us.

God rewards our faith. He responds to our diligence. He makes note of our faithfulness. Yes, we're saved by grace. Yes, we're loved simply because He is love. But He rewards those who seek after Him. He honors those who obey Him.

I felt sure that God would rescue me from my storm sooner than He did, but I now see how perseverance has had a profound, maturing effect on me. Though I was after relief, God wanted me to have a reward for my faith. Though I longed for a break, He wanted me to have a breakthrough. Though my gaze often drifted toward my problems, God was training me to think of eternity.

Think Eternity

A. W. Tozer once penned this now-famous phrase: "What comes to mind when you think about God is the most important thing about you."

To the degree that we understand God's character, His goodness, and His strength, we will rightly interpret our battles, our blessings, and His purpose for our lives.

If we believe that life is short and eternity is long and that God is good even though life is hard, we'll learn the value of perseverance and the power of God's promises. They're there because we need them. Those promises are ours!

If we believe that we're on this troubled earth for a short season and for a very distinct purpose, we'll see the wisdom of developing a steadfast heart. We'll want to mature. We'll value the fruitful life.

> With God's *goodness* before us, we can live with our eyes on a reality that we can't yet *see*. We know it'll be worth it in the end. We'll live like we're *made* for another world because we really, truly are.

With God's goodness before us, we can live with our eyes on a reality that we can't yet see. We know it'll be worth it in the end. We'll live like we're made for another world because we really, truly are.

Since life on earth is short and eternity is long, let's spend some time pondering how this life affects the next.

Here's my paraphrase of what Chip Ingram shared one day on my radio show: "Heaven isn't a concept; it's a place with streets, buildings, sights, sounds, and colors. The minute the Christ-follower dies, he or she is ushered to heaven—absent from the body, present with the Lord. That dearly departed saint will be conscious, have feelings, and recognize loved ones and other believers who've gone before them." Imagine.

We will give physical hugs. We'll belly laugh. We'll sing new songs. Enjoy new creations. We'll feast with other believers. We'll share stories and learn more of God's faithfulness—what He provided and what He prevented. We'll forever enjoy the Lord, the Creator of heaven and earth. This sounds nothing like the never-ending, boring church service that so many imagine heaven will be.

Bestselling author and pastor John Burke has joined me on my radio show several times, and he has shared that heaven will be a sensory explosion. We'll see, hear, taste, touch, and smell wonders like we've never known before. Whatever delectable food we've tasted on earth is just a fore-taste of things to come. The sights, scents, and glimpses of God's creation here on earth—the things that take our breath away—they're just a glimmer of what's to come. He asked, "Do you think God saved His best work for earth?" He continued, "Most Christians know so little about heaven that they're more excited about retirement than they are about eternity."

He went on to say that "Earth is a compressed time capsule: tastes of heaven and tastes of hell mixed together. But one day, these two will separate." For the Christian, this means that what we've tasted of God's goodness will suddenly abound, flourish, and multiply. Many times over. We'll be absolutely surrounded by His goodness. We'll marvel at His attention to detail. We'll be undone by His very personal attention to our story.

And that's not all. What we've endured at the hands of the enemy during our time on earth will be wiped away, never to negatively impact us again. Every hurt healed. Every loss restored. Every lie swallowed up in truth. Never again will we be in the devil's crosshairs. Justice will be served, and he'll get what's coming to him.

Imagine eternity with Jesus, an explosion of God's goodness with no downside. No more tears, no more hurt, no more pain. Oh, the stories we will share with each other in heaven about how Jesus led us each safely home.

Anticipation Is Healthy and Essential

Did you know that anticipation is important for your soul, your brain, and your overall health? Think about how good it feels to look forward to vacations, holidays, and special outings. We anticipate, prepare, and prioritize as we look ahead to our special day. Sometimes the excitement we feel prior to the event exceeds the actual experience, but the anticipation is still remarkably healthy.

> Research has shown that anticipation is such a strong feeling, people are happier in the anticipation of a holiday than in remembering the actual experience. It is anticipation that is generating this happiness, this improved feeling of well-being. . . .
>
> The anticipation of failure when we have placed such great importance on something—like a perfect holiday turning out to be a worst nightmare—can overwhelm the positive impact it may have. But by developing the anticipatory experiences—the planning, knowing where we will eat, how we will travel, the history of the place we will visit—then we can counter any of these concerns. . . .
>
> Give yourself things to look forward to and the world will seem a brighter place.[3]

What if you decided to *look forward* to your next breakthrough? What if you looked to Jesus with anticipation, wholeheartedly believing that right this very moment He is up to something good for you? And what if you—even more earnestly—developed a holy anticipation for where and how you'll spend millions and millions of years in the presence of God, apart from the enemy, without pain and suffering. Can you picture it? Know this: Creation eagerly waits for that day when God recognizes you for who you really are—His beloved heir. Let's read what Scripture says:

> For all creation is waiting eagerly for that future day when God will reveal who his children really are.
>
> Romans 8:19

The extended quote above connects anticipation to feelings of well-being. But here's an important point: When we look forward with anticipation, our brain releases feel-good hormones, which physiologically helps to reinforce good behavior. Once again, science is gradually catching up with Scripture. Consider that as we look forward to eternity with Jesus, as we joyfully anticipate His return, our whole self—mind, body, and spirit—will be fully alive, fully engaged in preparation for that great day. And even our own physiology will support God's desire for us to live ready.

The Life to Come

Life on earth is as bad as it gets for those of us who trust and follow Christ. Every tear, Jesus collects. Every act of obedience, every generous gift, every heartfelt sacrifice, every passionate prayer prayed in the privacy of your heart, God has been there. He's made note of it. Jesus will one day surprise you with His goodness and His meticulous attention to detail.

> *Jesus will one day surprise you with His goodness and His meticulous attention to detail.*

There's not a moment of your life that has escaped His notice. That time you sobbed on your bathroom floor? He was there with you. And when you got up, washed your face, and headed out the door to face your day? That's called perseverance, and He rewards such things.

When I decided to learn more about heaven, rewards, and God's desire for faithful stewardship, I was surprised to hear a number of Christians say things like, "Oh, I don't bother myself with thoughts on rewards. Jesus is enough." Or, "I'm not going to make it about what I receive. That sounds like the prosperity gospel." Or, "I don't think there's anything to that whole rewards things. Heaven with Jesus will be enough."

Jesus *is* more than enough and would be more than enough if our inheritance stopped right there. And yet, by His sacrifice and victory on the cross, Jesus more than saved us; He made us joint heirs with Him.[4]

Follow Him through the Gospels and you'll see Him talk about stewardship, multiplication, and rewards. We've become heirs of a kingdom not just in status but also for a purpose. There are realities of the kingdom that God wants us to appropriate, walk in, and steward for the greater good of the story He's writing on the earth today, which will profoundly affect His eternal kingdom (who's there, how we live, etc.).

If these things matter enough to Jesus to talk about, they need to matter enough for us to learn about. Read these very specific words to us:

> Do not lay up for yourselves treasures on earth, where moth and rust destroy and where thieves break in and steal; *but lay up for yourselves treasures in heaven*, where neither moth nor rust destroys and where thieves do not break in and steal. For where your treasure is, there your heart will be also.
>
> Matthew 6:19–21 NKJV (emphasis mine)

If Scripture speaks repeatedly of rewards, don't you think it's worth a deeper look? And if Jesus Himself said, "Store up for yourselves treasures in heaven," doesn't that imply some kind of action on our part? And if He said it, doesn't that make it important to us?

Picture this scenario with me, if you will. A young family decides to move to the inner city to make a difference among those in need. Mom asks the two sons to join her for a walk to see if they can meet some of the neighbors. The younger son says, "Hey, Mom! How about if we bake some bread and give fresh loaves to the neighbors we meet?" Mom thinks that's a great idea. Meanwhile, she notices her older son camped in front of the TV, not moving. She asks him to get up and get moving. He just looks over his shoulder and sweetly says, "Aw, Mom. No thanks. It's enough just to be in your family."

Jesus *is* enough. He didn't save us to slave us. He saved us because He loves us. And because we love Him, we learn what He cares about and we live accordingly.

We're saved by grace, but we're rewarded for our stewardship.

Why does it matter that we live the kind of life that God rewards? Because what God rewards reveals what's especially close to His heart (which to me also reflects His unfathomable character and goodness).

God loves it when we

- Seek *first* the kingdom of God[5]
- Tend to the poor[6]
- Steward our call[7]
- Refresh others[8]
- Give sacrificially and generously[9]
- Forgive and love[10]
- Pray[11]
- Suffer well[12]
- Persevere[13]
- Preach the Word of God, lead in a godly way[14]
- Follow Christ[15]

When we live like the kingdom people we were always meant to be, when we tend to matters close to God's heart, He rewards us both in this life and the next. Why? Because our lives shout to a world in need, *THIS! This is what God is like!*

God so loves the world that He wants us, as His representatives, to reflect His heart to those who would love and trust Him if they knew Him.

> The Lord isn't really being slow about his promise, as some people think. No, he is being patient for your sake. He does not want anyone to be destroyed, but wants everyone to repent.
>
> 2 Peter 3:9

An Upside-Down Kingdom

There's a very important day ahead of us. And based on Scripture, some Christians will suffer great loss when they appear before the judgment seat of Christ.[16] Their life's work will be placed upon the altar. Their ambitions, self-promotions, their prideful posturing, and their pretend praying. And it will *all* burn up. Scripture says they will be like someone barely escaping the flames. Saved, but with nothing to show for it. Imagine.

This makes my knees quake. Especially in a culture that celebrates celebrity Christianity. We aspire to it. Reward it. Are jealous of it. And all the while, much of the kingdom thrives in the nooks and crannies of life, out of the public eye.

How much angst have we allowed in our souls because our perspective of God's kingdom mirrored that of our high school experience? You've got the few privileged popular peeps, and the rest just sit around and wish they were somebody else.

But what if we recaptured a fresh picture of what Christ values? What if we had a stronger sense of what He rewards? What if we really started to believe that this coming kingdom has nothing to do with numbers or celebrity and everything to do with faith, hope, and love?

What if we broke free from posturing for popularity and instead learned to love our *actual lives* and decided to live them well?

I'll tell you what would happen. We'd start to know a joy and contentment we never thought possible. We'd see the value of extended time around our tables. Our neighbors might witness us as peaceful and not in a hurry. I think we'd give more funds to missions and probably be more kind to and grateful for our pastors.

I think we'd find it our great honor to visit the shut-in and the prisoner, to help the single parent and the elderly neighbor. And I think we'd feel such a sacredness in our service that we'd be tempted to look around for angels in our midst. I think we'd pause a little longer when we pray for our food, or when we notice a sunset, or after someone shares her heart. I'm pretty sure we'd start to take ourselves less seriously and God much more seriously.

We'd start to see the value of an offering given in faith. We'd quit comparing ourselves to others because we finally know that no one can fill the space that God has assigned to us. We'd pray for the popular, but pity them too, because they have their own crosses to bear.

I think that once we got ahold of God's heart for this world, and we saw how excited He is to reward our faith-steps, we'd want to live our whole lives in faith. We'd make risk-taking a normal part of life. We'd give in ways that make us blush because we now know there's no out-giving God. I think we'd become audacious, inside and out. And amazingly, I think we'd be content to be misunderstood because we'd finally know and believe that man's opinion changes like the weather, and we're made for better things.

Since such a great cloud of witness surrounds us, I pray we will throw off everything that hinders and slows us down and the sin that continually trips us up so we can run the race God has set before us. Jesus did. He paved the way. Now we follow in His footsteps. He is with us. He is for us. And He moves on every act prompted by our faith. Our faith is priceless to Him.

Yes, we have a target on our back. Yes, the enemy has our number. Yes, he knows what schemes have worked on us in the past. But what he doesn't know is that we're different now. God is healing us from the inside out. What worked on us before won't work next time. We know how to fight now. We know how to stand. We know what faith does for our heart. God is shoring us up.

We're getting wise to the enemy's schemes. We're quicker to discern a lie. We won't put up with the absence of peace. And we're done messing around with thoughts of insecurity and inferiority. We're learning to live with eternity in mind. We know that our offerings to God are absolutely secure with Him. Nobody can touch one iota of what we've entrusted to Jesus.

So yes, the enemy is after us, but far more important to us is that God is *for* us. Nothing can separate us from His love. He's the one who is able to keep us from falling, to present us before His glorious presence—without fault, and with great joy.

He's gone ahead to prepare a place for us. He says that our finite minds cannot begin to grasp all He has prepared for those of us who belong to Him.

Soon and very soon, Jesus is coming again for us. Scripture says that all of creation groans for that day when God reveals who His children really are. So we live like the kingdom people we are. Bold. Faith-filled. Audacious. And true. Jesus is coming, and He *wants* to reward us for the life we lived on earth.

> Yet what we suffer now is nothing compared to the glory he will reveal to us later. For all creation is waiting eagerly for that future day when God will reveal who his children really are.
>
> Romans 8:18–19

And so, dear friends, while you are waiting for these things to happen, make every effort to be found living peaceful lives that are pure and blameless in his sight.

2 Peter 3:14

To live with eternity in mind means that we can find redemptive value in every step we take. We won't get everything we want when we want it down here, but we won't know what to do with all God is, all He's preparing for us when life on earth is through.

In his stunning book *All Things New*, John Eldredge asks this question:

What would you love your reception into the kingdom to be? You should put some words to that, given how important it is. A friend of mine who has labored long in the Great War with evil shared his vision with me in a moment of tender vulnerability:

"I want to finish well. I want to return as a hero, a warrior worthy of the kingdom. I had this vision—I don't know if it was an actual vision or just my heart's expression. I saw myself, sword at my side, shield slung over my back, making my way up the main street of the City. I wore the battle gear of war, soiled by long years at the front. People lined both sides of the street to welcome me, the great cloud, I guess; I recognized hundreds of faces, the faces of those whose freedom I fought for. Their smiles and tears filled my heart with profound joy. As I made my way up the street toward Jesus and our Father, my friends and fellow warriors stepped into the street with me, and we moved forward as a band. I saw angels there, maybe angels who fought for us and with us, walking alongside. I saw flower petals on the pavement; I saw banners flapping in the breeze. We reached the throne and knelt. Jesus came forward and kissed my forehead, and we embraced deeply, freely, like I always knew we would. Then my Father stepped forward and took me by the shoulders and said, 'Well done, my son. Very well done indeed. Welcome home.' As we embraced, a great cheer went up from the crowd."

Now, *that* would be a reception worth living for. *The reality that every story will be told rightly should affect your choices today.* If there is no cost to our

Christian faith, how then shall we be rewarded? And may I point out that if we, too, would love to receive a hero's welcome, it helps to keep in mind that valiant deeds require desperate times. The desperate times are all around us, friends; now for the valiant deeds.[17]

What kind of hero's welcome awaits you? Can you imagine it? How, then, shall we live?

We enjoy deep intimacy with God right now because we can. We abide in His presence and we do what He says. We keep His Word especially close to our heart. We keep marching. We pray God's Word. We dream wild dreams with Him. We take crazy faith risks. We believe. We encourage each other. We love well. We reflect His heart to the least of these. We remind one another that this is not our home. We're only passing through. But we make this journey for a purpose.

Every step counts.

So we urge one another onward and upward. We remind ourselves that Jesus does His best work in our weakness. He loves our faith. And He's happily at work, preparing a place for us. I think it's safe to say He's downright giddy for that day. And our hearts beat strong at the thought of the welcome and the life that await us.

I pray you've found some healing on this journey. I pray your heart is encouraged and your faith strengthened. And I pray God will continue to work such wonders in and through you that countless others will look to Him for their own story.

It's been my great honor to travel this road with you.

Until we meet again.

Susie Larson

Put It into Practice

Focus on . . .

Looking Forward with Expectancy

Scripture Says . . .

But as the Scriptures say,

> No eye has ever seen and no ear has ever heard
>> and it has never occurred to the human heart
> All the things God prepared for those who love Him.

God has shown us these profound and startling realities through His Spirit. The Spirit searches all things, even the deep mysteries of God.

1 Corinthians 2:9–10 THE VOICE

Science Says . . .

Anticipating events has been shown to be more enjoyable than anticipating material goods, such as a new phone. This explains why buying theater tickets for the summer, making restaurant reservations for next Christmas, or booking a flight some months ahead can give us a feeling of positivity.[18]

Pursue Healing

If you find yourself looking back with regret more than you look forward with expectancy, memorize some passages on God's grace,

His love, and His unending compassion. Read some books on heaven. Imagine what your hero's welcome will be like. And start living *now* with eternity in mind.

Pray for a Miracle

Father in heaven, I want my life to count for eternity! It doesn't matter where I've been, it matters where I'm going and that I get to spend forever with You! Give me a sense of the eternal opportunities right in front of me. Open my eyes to the evidences of Your movement all around me. Make my heart beat again for the things You care about. Remind me daily that life on earth is short but eternity is long. I have so much to look forward to. Help me live on the earth today like Your promises are true. Transform me into the person I never imagined but that You always dreamed I would be. In Your name I pray. Amen.

Soul Searching

In what area of life do you most long to see God's redemption and reward?

_____

_____

_____

_____

_____

_____

_____

> Dear Father in heaven, through Christ Jesus, You have raised me to NEW life in Him! Help me to lift my gaze and to set my sights on the realities of heaven where Jesus now sits in His place of honor at God's right hand. Help me, Lord, to prioritize eternal things more than I do earthly things. Thank You, Lord, that by Your power and resurrection, I have officially died to this life, and my real life is now hidden with Christ. And thank You, God, there's a day coming when Christ will be revealed for all the world to see, and at that time I will share in His amazing glory. Help me live unselfishly and faithfully because Your word is true. Amen.
>
> Colossians 3:1–4 (paraphrase)

Prayer

Father, You are greater than I know, more powerful than I can imagine. That You—the Creator of the unnumbered galaxies—would look upon me with such love and interest . . . well, it brings me to my knees. Forgive me for the countless times I've lived and strived as if my earthly concerns are all that matter. Yet You delight in every detail of my life. Everything has a spiritual component to You. Help me let that in. Open my eyes to see You in the everyday-ness of my life. Fill me afresh with Your Holy Spirit and awaken my heart to be a flow-through account of blessing from Your heart to the world around me. Let us see Your miracles once again, Lord! Let our children see Your glory at work! Do wonders in our midst and miracles in our hearts. Heal us in ways we never thought possible. Heal through us in ways that will change the world. Thank You, Jesus. In Your name I pray. Amen.

Life Reflection

1. What rises up in you when you think of God's desire to reward you for the ways you've loved and served Him? Write down your thoughts.

2. In what area of your life do you see the most fruit?

3. In what area of your life have you most valiantly persevered? Maybe you don't see the kind of fruit you'd like, but you're still standing.

4. Can you imagine God rewarding you for your willingness to persevere? What do you think He wants to say to you about your staying power?

5. What kind of hero's welcome do you want to receive? How do you want your kingdom story to play out? Give some thought to this one.

Spiritual Reset

Picture your homecoming, the moment when all of eternity and all the angels and saints pause for you. Heaven will hush as you stand before your Savior to hear Him say, "Well done, good and faithful servant!" And then heaven will erupt with welcome and celebration as you accept the incorruptible crown that Jesus is reserving for you. It will be your unique moment to bless the heart of God. On that day, you will prove that you valued Jesus' death for you, and you gave Him your heart and life in return. God wants that day, when unseen and eternal things become visible, to be the most wonderful day of your life.[19]

PRAISE—Acronym Exercise

P—Praise Him. Write out a prayer of thanksgiving just because He is God.

_____

_____

_____

R—Remember and Repent. Write out a memory of God's faithfulness. Spend time with Him and repent of anything He brings to mind.

_____

_____

_____

A—Ask Him for what's on your heart.

I—Intercede for others.

S—Stand on God's promises. Write out a promise that under-girds what you're asking Him for.

E—Eternity. Put your life, your burdens, and your prayer list up to the lens of eternity. Ask Jesus to help you look up and think long, with eternity in mind.

Digging Deeper

*Use your journal or notebook for this section.

A. Read 1 Corinthians 15:35–58 and note the distinction between the bodies we have now and the bodies we'll inherit. Write out a prayer asking God for an eternal perspective on the body you have now. Ponder the truth that someday you'll no longer battle chronic fatigue, headaches, cellulite, or insomnia. A better day is coming for you!

B. Revisit verse 58 in the passage above. Note the three operative words in this passage: *strong, immovable, enthusiastic* (might be different ones depending on your translation). Grab a dictionary and/or thesaurus and expound on these words. Rewrite verse 58 as a personalized paraphrase.

C. Prayerfully read Revelation 21:1–7 and write down the things that will pass away and what will take their place.

D. Read 1 John 3:1–3 and notice how our very hope in Him *purifies us*. We will one day see Him, and we will be like Him. What in your life blocks your view of Him? What do you need to do to find perspective again? Write down your thoughts.

E. Consider the fact that the Creator of the Universe is making preparations for you right now. Consider too the brevity of life on earth and the enormity of God's goodness that awaits us on the other side. Write out a prayer and ask the Lord to stir up your sense of anticipation and to give you a God-sized, rewardable vision for the rest of your life.

Find the following downloadable print at SusieLarson.com.

BECAUSE I KNOW GOD IS
POWERFUL & GOOD,

I WILL

pursue wholeness and pray for a miracle.

I WILL

face my battles with a heart of faith.

I WILL

carry my blessings with fierce accountability.

I WILL

steward my calling with holy conviction.

I WILL

live with eternity in mind.

Your Christian life is to be a continuous proof that God works impossibilities. Your Christian life is to be a series of impossibilities *made possible* and actual by God's almighty power.[20]

Acknowledgments

TO ANDY MCGUIRE ~ You're more than an editor, you've become a good friend. There's one moment I'll not forget. I'd just come off the battlefield, weary, worn out, and with scribbled notes in my hand. But I was in no shape to make sense of them. You did that for me. If the timing of this book feels divine to anyone, it's because of *your* initiative, investment, and wisdom. Thank you for all that you do behind the scenes to move God's purposes forward. Appreciate you so much!

To Carra Carr ~ I first met you as the Marketing Director for Bethany House Publishers. But then we became fast friends. Thank you for your willingness to review my rough draft and for pushing me to be a better writer. And for sharing your beautiful heart with me. I love you, friend!

To Jeff Braun ~ You're the one who first reached out to me on behalf of BHP. Look what God has done! I am forever grateful. I love your humble, unassuming way, Jeff. And somehow you manage to preserve my voice and make the project sing. I so appreciate you! Thank you for your friendship!

To the leadership at Bethany House Publishers ~ Thank you for your unwavering commitment to God's Word. Can't tell you what a joy it is to partner with you!

To Leslie Wilson ~ Thank you for your editorial advice. Appreciate you!

To Shaun, Grace, and Chandler ~ Thanks for your constant support, prayers, and hard work. Appreciate you so much!

To my sample readers ~ Lynn, Pam, Bonnie, Judy, Bev, Karen, Summer, Kelly, Andie, Daryl, Tabby, Lynette, Jane, Carol, Tamra, Karna, Kathy, and Jane. Thank you for giving your time to this process. May Jesus redeem every moment for you!

To Tara Jenkins for her beautiful artwork and decorative downloads. Appreciate you!

To Kaitlyn Bouchillon for your help in organizing my notes. Bless you!

To Steph for walking me through my great unearthing process. I just love you!

To my kids ~ Jake, Lizzie, Luke, Kristen, Jordan, Jiethyl, and baby Lachlan. We love you so very much. May Jesus continue to work wonders in your life! May we all live with eternity in mind.

To Kev ~ I'll never have enough words to express how profoundly grateful I am for you. Thank you for loving me the way Jesus loves His church. I am who I am because of the way you've modeled Christ's love to me. Thank you, honey.

Notes

Introduction

1. "Metabolizing our hurts" is a term used by speaker and author Dr. Jim Wilder.

Chapter 1 He Restores

1. John Eldredge, *All Things New* (Nashville: Thomas Nelson, 2017), 16–17.

2. Rick Hanson, quoted in *Battle Ready* by Kelly Balarie (Grand Rapids, MI: Baker Books, 2018), 20–21, emphasis mine.

3. David Chadwick, *From Superficial to Significant* (Eugene, OR: Harvest House, 2017), 40.

Chapter 2 My Soul and Body Ache

1. Steve Farrar, *Manna* (Nashville: Thomas Nelson, 2016), 67.

2. If you're dealing with these sorts of things, pick up my book *The Uncommon Woman*. I pray it encourages you!

3. See John 8:32.

4. Jan Silvious, *Courage for the Unknown Season* (Colorado Springs: NavPress, 2017), 27, 33.

5. Anthony Komaroff, "The Gut-Brain Connection," Harvard Health Publishing, www .health.harvard.edu/diseases-and-conditions/the-gut-brain-connection.

6. Many people who've struggled with brain fog, fatigue, intestinal discomfort, joint pain, or anxiety have found relief simply by omitting corn, gluten, sugar, or dairy from their diet. It's worth a try!

7. See THE VOICE translation of this psalm. It's beautiful.

8. Mark Batterson, *Whisper* (Sisters, OR: Multnomah, 2017), 2.

9. See Hebrews 12:1–2.

10. These wise words came from my mentor, Bonnie Newberg. They ring in my ears throughout every battle.

11. See John 8:44.

Chapter 3 I'm Afraid

1. Jennifer Kennedy Dean, *Live a Praying Life Without Fear* (Birmingham, AL: New Hope Publishers, 2016), 13–14.
2. Dean, *Live a Praying Life Without Fear.*
3. Dr. Timothy Jennings has shared this insight several times on my radio show.
4. See Ephesians 6:16.
5. Nik Ripken (pseudonym), an expert on the persecuted church, has said this more than once as a guest on my radio show.
6. See Daniel 3 for a biblical example of an "even if" prayer.
7. Dr. Timothy Jennings, *The God-Shaped Brain* (Downers Grove, IL: IVP Books, 2013), 45–47.
8. Prayerfully ask the Lord to show you if this fear is connected to a childhood trauma. Consider working this through with a counselor, spiritual director, or mentor.
9. Carter Conlon, *Fear Not* (Ventura, CA: Regal Books, 2012), 127.

Chapter 4 I Feel Guilty and Ashamed

1. Christa Black Gifford, *Heart Made Whole* (Grand Rapids, MI: Zondervan, 2016), 175.
2. Dr. Bessel van der Kolk, *The Body Keeps the Score* (New York: Penguin Books, 2014), 53.
3. L. B. Cowman, *Streams in the Desert* (Grand Rapids, MI: Zondervan, 1997), October 4 reading.
4. If you're not a fan of *The Message* paraphrase, look up this passage in your favorite translation and spend some time with it. We are living, breathing miracles because of what Christ has done!
5. Dr. Curt Thompson, *The Soul of Shame* (Downers Grove, IL: IVP Books, 2015), 46–47, 50, emphasis mine.
6. Aubrey Sampson, *Overcomer* (Grand Rapids, MI: Zondervan, 2015), 106.

Chapter 5 I Feel Anxious and Worried

1. Max Lucado, *Anxious for Nothing* (Nashville: Thomas Nelson, 2017), 103.
2. For some, anxiety is a result of chemical imbalance and may require medication, so see your doctor!
3. Psalm 91:4.
4. Strong's Interlinear Bible Search, Psalm 46:10, Studylight.org.
5. Ibid.
6. Robert Morgan, *Worry Less, Live More* (Nashville: Thomas Nelson, 2017), 101.
7. Read the story in Matthew 8.
8. Dr. Carol Peters-Tanksley, *Overcoming Fear and Anxiety Through Spiritual Warfare* (Lake Mary, FL: Siloam, 2017), 76–78, emphasis mine.
9. Strong's Interlinear Bible Search, John 14:27, Studylight.org.
10. Insights from a back-and-forth conversation with my friend Carra Carr.
11. See Romans 8:17.
12. Strong's Interlinear Bible Search, Psalm 23:5, Studylight.org.
13. Trevin Wax, *Feasting as an Act of War,* The Gospel Coalition Blog, April 24, 2017, https://www.thegospelcoalition.org/blogs/trevin-wax/feasting-as-an-act-of-war/.
14. Strong's Interlinear Bible Search, Isaiah 40:31, Studylight.org.
15. Larry Crabb, as quoted in Dee Brestin's book *He Calls You Beautiful* (Colorado Springs: Multnomah, 2017), 174.
16. Peters-Tanksley, *Overcoming Fear and Anxiety*, 18.

17. Kelly Balarie, *Battle Ready* (Grand Rapids, MI: Baker Books, 2018), 25.

18. Steve Farrar, *Manna* (Nashville: Thomas Nelson, 2016), 95.

Chapter 6 I'm Grieving

1. Linda Barrick, *Beauty Marks* (Colorado Springs: David C. Cook, 2017), 25.

2. F. B. Meyer quote taken from *Streams in the Desert* (Grand Rapids, MI: Zondervan, 1997), 294.

3. Barrick, *Beauty Marks*, 25–31.

4. Dr. Timothy Jennings, *The God-Shaped Brain* (Downers Grove, IL: IVP Books, 2013), 56, emphasis mine.

5. Christa Black Gifford, *Heart Made Whole* (Grand Rapids, MI: Zondervan, 2016), 176.

6. Gina Stepp, "Give Sorrow More Than Words," Vison.org, winter 2007, http://www.vision.org/visionmedia/grief-and-loss/neuroscience/2166.aspx.

7. Stefan Klein, as quoted in Gina Stepp, "Give Sorrow More Than Words."

8. Jan Silvious said this to me on my radio show. We talked about her book *Courage for the Unknown Season*.

Chapter 7 I'm Discouraged

1. Nika Maples, *Hunting Hope* (Franklin, TN: Worthy Publishing, 2016), 227.

2. This story originally appeared in my book *Your Powerful Prayers* (Minneapolis: Bethany House, 2016)

3. Larson, *Your Powerful Prayers*, 127.

4. See 2 Corinthians 1:20.

5. If searching Scripture for a promise feels intimidating to you, check out David Wilkerson's book *The Jesus Person Promise Book*.

6. Roy Hession, *Calvary Road* (Fort Washington, PA: CLC Publications, 1950), 28.

7. Lance Hahn, *The Master's Mind* (Nashville: Thomas Nelson, 2017), 19, 2.

8. Carolyn Gregoire, "The Science of Conquering Your Fears," December 6, 2017, Huffington Post, https://www.huffingtonpost.com/2013/09/15/conquering-fear_n_3909020.html.

9. Christa Black Gifford, *Heart Made Whole*, 117.

Chapter 8 I'm Insecure

1. Mark Batterson, *Whisper* (Colorado Springs: Multnomah, 2017), 2.

2. Bo Stern, *Ruthless* (Colorado Springs: NavPress, 2014), 124.

3. Susie Larson, *The Uncommon Woman* (Chicago: Moody Publishers, 2008), 46–47, 111.

4. Dr. Timothy Jennings, *The God-Shaped Brain*, 156.

5. John Eldredge, *All Things New* (Nashville: Nelson, 2017), 119.

Chapter 9 I'm Selfish

1. Dr. Jim Wilder, *Joyful Journey* (East Peoria, IL: Life Model Works, 2015), 18.

2. See Philippians 1:21.

3. *Life Application Study Bible: New Living Translation*, 2nd ed. (Carol Stream, IL: Tyndale House Publishers, 2004), 1 Samuel 9 study notes, emphasis mine.

4. Strong's Interlinear Bible Search, Studylight.org.

5. Keren Peters-Atkinson, "Warning: Selfishness is Bad for Your Health," Monday Mornings With Madison, September 3, 2013, http://mondaymornings.madisoncres.com/warning-selfishness-is-bad-for-your-health/.

Notes

6. Dr. Timothy Jennings, *The God-Shaped Brain*, 33.

7. Bo Stern, *Ruthless*, 88.

Chapter 10 He Rewards

1. Bruce Wilkinson, *A Life God Rewards* (Sisters, OR: Multnomah, 2002), 27.

2. See Psalm 127:2.

3. Nigel Holt, PhD, "Looking Forward to Things Is Good for You, So Plan for Your Next Treat," *The Conversation*, February 19, 2018, http://theconversation.com/looking-forward-to-things-is-good-for-you-so-plan-for-your-next-treat-91103.

4. See Romans 8:17.

5. Matthew 6:33; Matthew 19:29; 1 Corinthians 3:11–15; 2 Corinthians 5:9–10.

6. Proverbs 19:17; Luke 12:33–34; Matthew 25:35–40.

7. Matthew 6:3–4; Matthew 25:20–23; Luke 19:15–19; 1 Corinthians 3:8; Ephesians 6:8; 1 Timothy 6:18–19.

8. Hebrews 6:10; Proverbs 11:25; Mark 9:41.

9. Luke 6:38; 2 Corinthians 9:6.

10. Matthew 6:14–15; Luke 6:35; Colossians 1:13–14; Micah 7:18–19; Mark 11:25.

11. Matthew 6:6; Matthew 7:7–11; Luke 18:1–8.

12. Matthew 5:1–12; Luke 6:23; 2 Timothy 4:1–8.

13. Matthew 16:27; Colossians 1:11–12; Galatians 6:9; 2 Timothy 4:1–8; Revelation 2:10; 22:12.

14. 1 Peter 5:1–5; 2 Timothy 4:1–8.

15. John 14:3; 1 John 3:2; 1 Corinthians 15:42–44; Philippians 3:20–21.

16. See 1 Corinthians 3.

17. Eldredge, *All Things New*, 125–127, emphasis mine.

18. Holt, "Looking Forward to Things Is Good for You, So Plan for Your Next Treat."

19. Wilkinson, *A Life God Rewards*, 117.

20. Andrew Murray, *Absolute Surrender* (New Kensington, PA: Whitaker House, 1981/1982), 69, emphasis mine.

Susie Larson is a popular media voice, author, and national speaker. For eight years she hosted her own daily talk show, *Live the Promise with Susie Larson*. A veteran of the fitness field, Susie has also served as a media voice for Moody Radio and was the former cohost for Focus on the Family's daily live talk show, *Everyday Relationships with Dr. Greg Smalley*. Her passion is to see women and men everywhere strengthened in their faith and mobilized to live out their high calling in Jesus Christ.

Susie has twice been voted a top-ten finalist for the John C. Maxwell Transformational Leadership Award. This award recognizes people who go beyond themselves to make a positive impact in the lives of others. Her previous books include *Your Powerful Prayers, Your Beautiful Purpose, Your Sacred Yes, Growing Grateful Kids, The Uncommon Woman, Blessings for the Evening,* and *Blessings for the Morning.*

Susie and her husband, Kevin, live near Minneapolis, Minnesota, and have three adult sons, three beautiful daughters-in-law, one amazing grandson, and one adorable pit bull. For more information, visit susielarson.com.

More Wisdom and Inspiration from Susie!

Visit susielarson.com for more information.

Respond today to that nudge in your spirit—that desire to use your gifts and passions more fully in God's work—and discover God's beautiful purpose for your life.

Your Beautiful Purpose

It's so easy to give away our time to things un-appointed by God. In this practical and liberating book, Susie invites you to say no to overcommitment and yes to the life of joy, passion, and significance God has for you.

Your Sacred Yes

Through personal stories and biblical insights, Susie Larson shares the secrets to effective prayer in this warm and wise book. You'll be amazed at what your prayers can do when you combine reverence, expectation, and a tenacious hold on God's promises. Discover how to pray specifically and persistently with faith and joy!

Your Powerful Prayers

Blessings from Susie Larson

Visit susielarson.com for more information.

Start and end each day with an uplifting reminder of God's promises, love, and purpose for you. Instead of focusing on your worries and concerns, replace them with these daily doses of encouragement rooted in God's Word.

Blessings for the Morning and Evening

Journaling is a wonderful way to draw near to God. With Scripture on one page and writing space on the other, this beautiful journal lets you record all your thoughts, questions, and prayers as you read the Psalms; there are even prompts from bestselling author Susie Larson for when you're not sure what to write. When you're done, you'll have an inspiring reminder of your time in God's Word.

Journaling Through the Psalms

BETHANYHOUSE